ADAM BRUCE
THOMSON

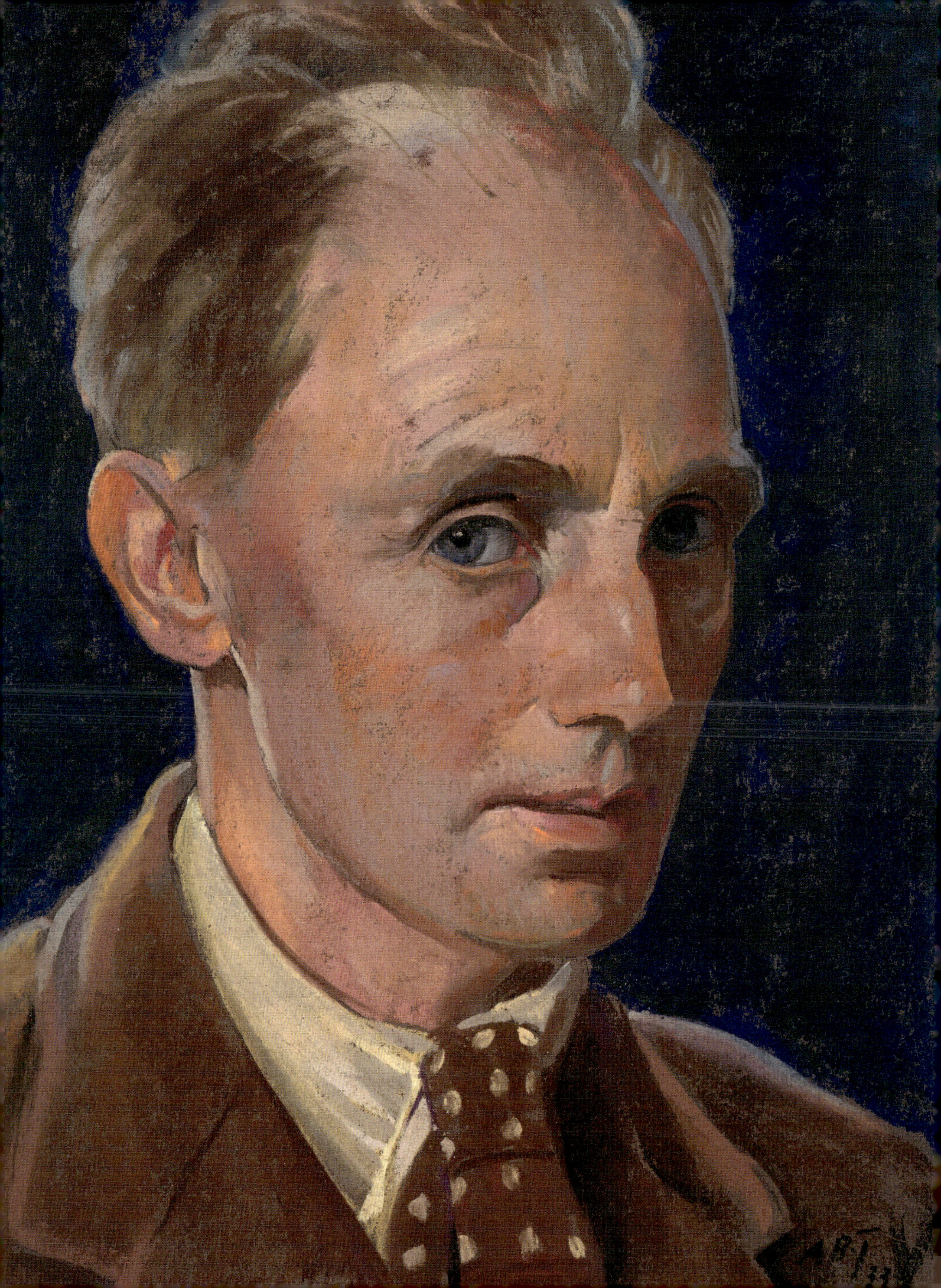

ADAM BRUCE THOMSON

THE QUIET PATH

DR HELEN E. SCOTT

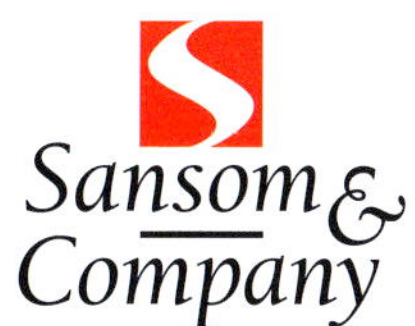

Sansom &
Company

First published in 2024 by Sansom and Company,
a publishing imprint of Redcliffe Press Ltd.,
81g Pembroke Road, Bristol BS8 3EA
www.sansomandcompany.co.uk | info@sansomandcompany.co.uk

ISBN 978-1-915670-14-4
© Text: The contributors
© Images: The artists

Published to coincide with the exhibition:
'Adam Bruce Thomson: The Quiet Path'
City Art Centre, Edinburgh
11 May–6 October 2024

British Library Cataloguing-in-Publication Data
A catalogue record for this book is available from the British Library.

Commissioning editor: Paul Deaton
Copyediting: Ann Kay
Design and typesetting: Melinda Welch, Design Deluxe, Bath
Printed and bound by Akcent Media

Front cover: Adam Bruce Thomson, *The Road to Ben Cruachan*, c.1932.
Private Collection. © The artist's estate. (Photograph: Antonia Reeve)

Rear cover: Adam Bruce Thomson, *North Bridge and Salisbury Crags, Edinburgh, from the
North West*, c.1934. City Art Centre, City of Edinburgh Museums and Galleries.
© The artist's estate. (Photograph: City Art Centre)

Frontispiece: Adam Bruce Thomson, *Self-Portrait*, 1933. National Galleries of Scotland.
Gift of Elizabeth Hall (née Hislop), the artist's great-niece, 2017.
© The artist's estate. (Photograph: National Galleries of Scotland)

CONTENTS

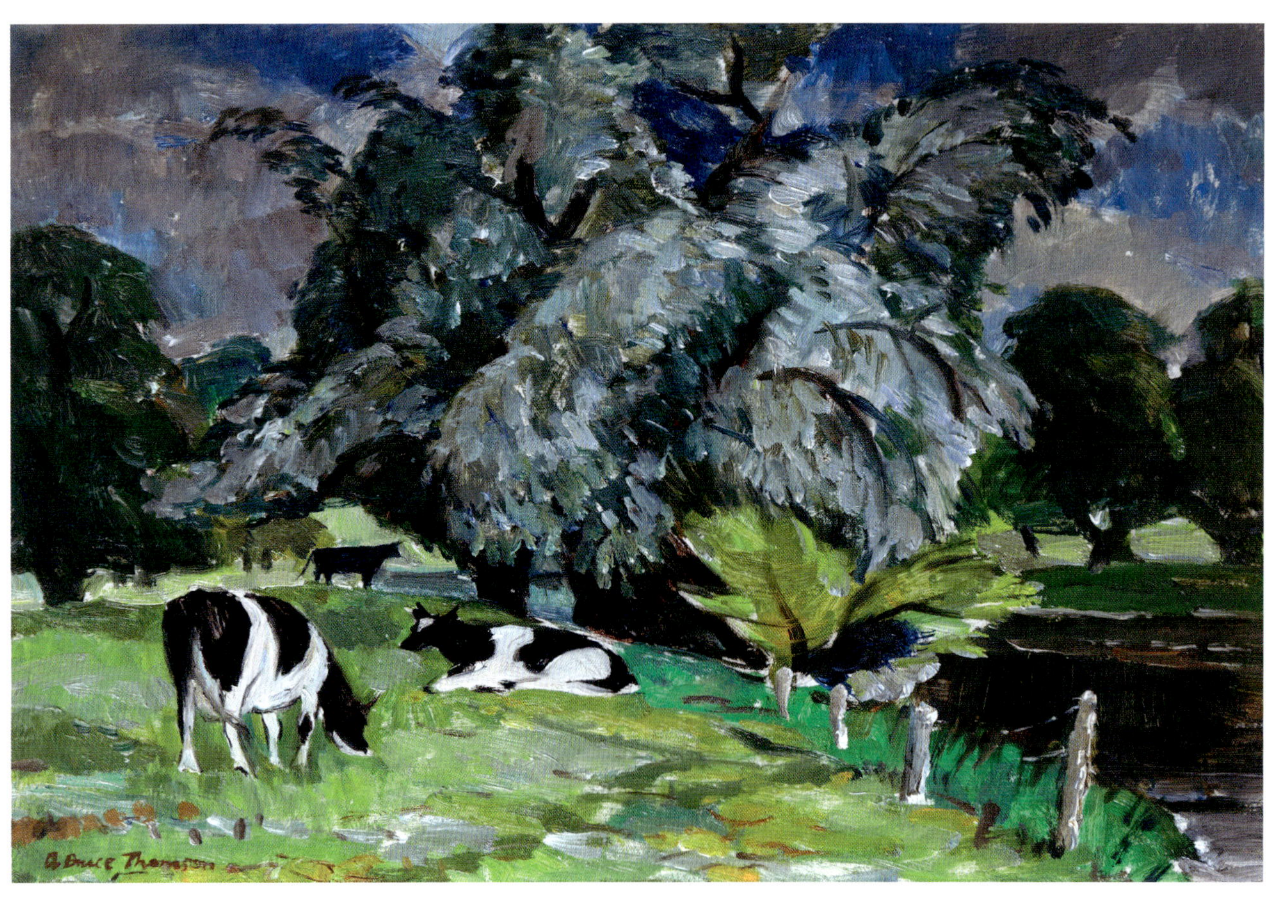

Adam Bruce Thomson, *Willow Trees, Cattle and River*, before 1967.
City Art Centre, City of Edinburgh Museums and Galleries. © The artist's estate.
(Photograph: City Art Centre)

FOREWORD   SIR ALEXANDER McCALL SMITH CBE

The personal discovery of an artist's work is a delight that will be familiar to anyone who takes an interest in art. I remember very clearly the pleasure I felt when, many years ago, I went to an Édouard Vuillard exhibition in London, not previously having paid much attention to his work. I felt a strong sense of being admitted to a vision that would change the way I looked at art and, through art, at the world about me. I felt the same when I began to pursue an interest in other artists, ranging from Poussin to Ravilious. Every personal discovery brought an enlargement of outlook and fresh satisfaction.

My enthusiasm for Adam Bruce Thomson arose as a result of an earlier interest I had in work done prior to the Second World War by a number of English artists, including Edward Bawden and Paul Nash. I was interested in artists who showed a high degree of skill in draughtsmanship, and who were also capable of capturing stillness. This had led me, of course, to James Cowie, one of my favourite painters, whose *A Portrait Group* (c.1933–40) is, in my view, one of the most beautiful, haunting paintings in Scotland's national collection. I wanted to find other Scottish painters whose work had the same feel about it, and it was in the course of that search that I came across a remarkable picture of a young woman in domestic garb, engaged in the household task of doing the laundry (*A Woman Washing Clothes*, mid-1920s, Pl. 14). There was something compelling about the painting, but I knew nothing of the artist, who was revealed to be Adam Bruce Thomson. My friend, Guy Peploe, to whom I turn whenever a detail of Scottish art needs clarification, was able to tell me something about him, and armed with this information, I set out to find out more about this comparatively little-known artist. The opportunity arose to see several more of his paintings, and it

was not long before I became a keen supporter of his work.

What do I like about Adam Bruce Thomson? First and foremost, I think, is his painterly skill. In days when the ability to capture reality in paint is being downplayed, it is refreshing to find an artist who so effortlessly transports us into a landscape or interior with just the right amount of suggestion. We are there at the artist's side, sharing in his sense of wonder, in his enjoyment of the beauty and harmony of what he is observing. This applies in so many of Thomson's works. He is the quiet, unobtrusive observer who invites us to see something that he wishes to share with us. He has an eye for beauty, which is a great artistic gift. His paintings are beautiful – a quality that remains important, no matter what other tasks are assigned to art. It is a good thing for an artist to do: to remind us of the beauty of the world about us. That task must survive, whatever emphasis comes to be placed on the duty of art to challenge or disturb.

But I feel inclined to return to the quietness. There is nothing strident in the work of this most accomplished artist. There is, by contrast, resolution, peace, and harmony – all of which are in somewhat short supply in our currently troubled world.

Attention to the work of Adam Bruce Thomson is long overdue and much welcomed. Helen Scott is to be thanked for reminding us of a very fine artist who has not received the attention he is undoubtedly due. This publication will help to restore him to the central place that he should occupy in the history of twentieth-century Scottish art. There is a good body of work in public collections for us to enjoy and to share with others. As Dr Scott writes, it will take us down a quiet path, but it is a lovely and rewarding one.

DR HELEN E. SCOTT

ADAM BRUCE THOMSON

THE QUIET PATH

Adam Bruce Thomson (1885–1976) retired from Edinburgh College of Art in the summer of 1950. Having passed his 65th birthday in February that year, he saw out the remainder of his teaching commitments as a Senior Lecturer in the School of Drawing and Painting before standing down at the end of the academic session. Thomson's departure was formally noted by the College in its 1949–50 Annual Report. In a brief paragraph under the heading 'Staff', the retirement was reported alongside that of an office typist, Miss Marjorie McMorine. The Board of Management expressed its 'warm appreciation' to both members of staff for their 'long and loyal service to the College', before moving on to other matters.[1]

The understated nature of this short statement was in keeping with Thomson's character; he was always modest about his own achievements. While someone else in his position might have been disappointed to find their retirement accompanied by so little official fanfare, Thomson was probably relieved. He would not have wanted any 'fuss'.

Leaving his teaching position was, nonetheless, a major event in the artist's professional life. It also marked the end of an era in terms of the history of the College. Thomson had been part

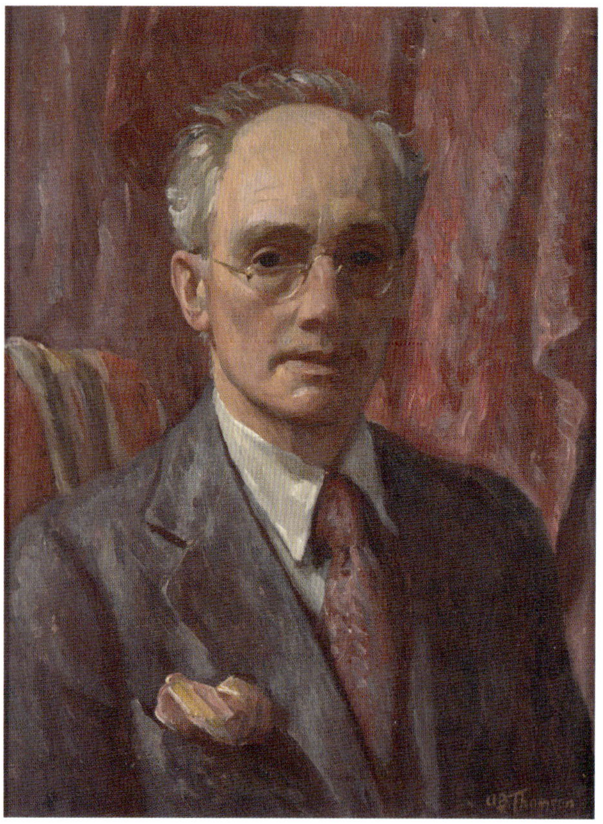

Fig. 1 Adam Bruce Thomson, *Self-Portrait*, c.1950. Private Collection. © The artist's estate. (Photograph: Antonia Reeve)

of the original cohort of students who trained at Edinburgh College of Art when it was first established in 1908. He went on to teach there for another forty years. When he retired, he was the final one of his generation to do so, the last tutor who could remember the building and its facilities as brand new.

Thomson's immediate colleagues recognised the significance of losing him. At the end of term, they presented him with a certificate bearing a message from the staff. Handwritten in calligraphic font, the certificate describes Thomson as an 'Artist, Teacher and Friend' whom they held in 'high regard'. It was given 'in appreciation of his long and happy association with us', with 'our most sincere good wishes for a long & successful retirement'.[2] This heartfelt message was followed by 46 staff signatures, including those of William Gillies, Penelope Beaton, William MacTaggart and Robin Philipson. Thomson was evidently touched by the gesture; he kept the certificate for the rest of his life.

Surviving personal artefacts like this provide a marked contrast to the perfunctory tone of official College documentation. Letters, photographs, diaries and notebooks, most of which are held in private collections, offer insights into a life of creativity, intellect and integrity. They attest to the affection and respect that Thomson inspired throughout his career, not only during his tenure at Edinburgh College of Art, but also in the productive decades that followed. His commitment to his chosen vocation was readily apparent to his peers. His contribution to the field of twentieth-century Scottish art was well recognised. Official institutional records only skim the surface. To those who knew him, Thomson was a talented artist, an impactful teacher and a loyal friend and family member.

Today, Adam Bruce Thomson's name receives noticeably less attention than others associated with the Edinburgh School.[3] Anne Redpath (1895–1965), William Gillies (1898–1973), William MacTaggart (1903–1981), John Maxwell (1905–1962) and Robin Philipson (1916–1992)

have all been extensively researched over the years and celebrated through publications and posthumous exhibitions. Thomson, by comparison, remains relatively neglected by art historians and curators, and accordingly overlooked by the wider public. He was perhaps less overtly ambitious than others in his circle, and his quiet, good-humoured demeanour meant that he tended not to make himself the centre of attention. This natural reticence, however, should not be interpreted as a lack of drive or vision. Thomson considered his art very seriously, working with remarkable dedication into his early nineties. Versatile and prolific, he created an outstandingly rich body of work – a little-known *oeuvre* that deserves to be explored.

EARLY YEARS

Adam Bruce Thomson was born in Edinburgh on 22 February 1885. His father, Adam Thomson senior, was a qualified cabinetmaker by profession, who rose through the ranks of a large furniture manufacturing firm in the city. His mother, Marion Thomson (née Ritchie), was originally from the village of Oxton in Berwickshire. Adam was the couple's third child. His siblings included elder sisters Marion (b. 1880) and Margaret (b. 1882), younger sister Mary (b. 1888) and younger brother Thomas (b. 1891). The family believed in the values of education and Christian faith, and as a boy Adam sang in the choir of St Mary's Episcopal Cathedral.[4] By all accounts it was a happy upbringing.

The Thomsons raised their children in the Dalry area of Edinburgh, south-west of the city centre. Records show that during Adam's infancy they lived on Caledonian Crescent. By the time of the 1901 Census they had moved to the nearby address of 13 Richmond Terrace, and shortly afterwards they set up home at 62 Dalry Road, where they remained until at least 1911.[5] Later, the household relocated to the relatively quieter surroundings of Polwarth, on the other side of the Union Canal.

Following in his father's footsteps, Thomson demonstrated creative inclinations from a young age. Among the earliest surviving examples of his work is a meticulously executed study of a pattern for floor tiling, dated 20 November 1899 (Fig. 2). Thomson would have been 14 years old at the time. At this stage, he was attending evening classes at Heriot-Watt College on Chambers Street, and it is possible that this design was produced in response to a set exercise. Thomson's parents may have expected him to enter the family profession of cabinetmaking.[6] The Art Department at Heriot-Watt College was originally orientated towards training students in a range of practical craft disciplines. Indeed, according to the 1901 Census, at the age of 16 Thomson was already employed as an 'apprentice furniture draughtsman'. Yet this apprenticeship was seemingly short-lived. Within a few years, he was putting his drawing skills to an altogether different purpose.

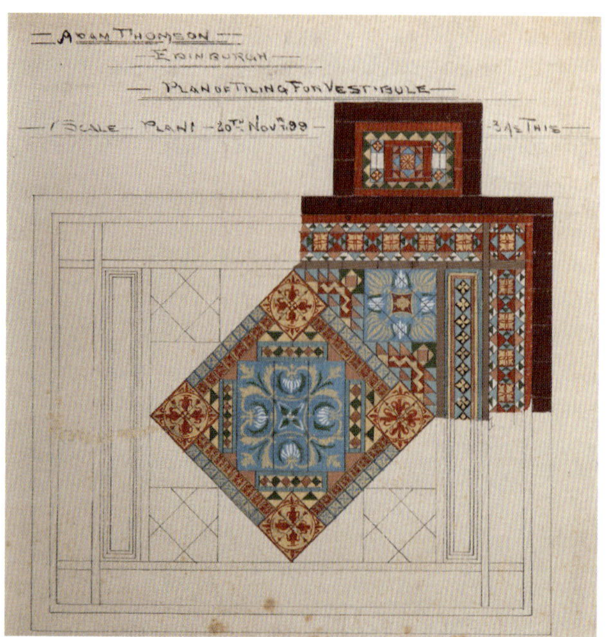

Fig. 2 Adam Bruce Thomson, *Plan of Tiling for Vestibule*, 1899. Private Collection. © The artist's estate. (Photograph: The Scottish Gallery)

ARTISTIC TRAINING ON THE MOUND

In the autumn of 1903 Thomson enrolled as a student at the Trustees' School of Art.[7] This teaching institution had been founded in 1760 by the Board of Trustees for Fisheries, Manufactures and Improvements in Scotland. Initially known as the Trustees' Drawing Academy, its founding purpose was to advance industrial design in Scotland, but over the years this focus shifted towards the provision of training in both the fine and applied arts. Like Heriot-Watt College, it operated according to the centralised South Kensington system of arts education, under the aegis of the Science and Art Department in London. By 1903 it had also assumed responsibility for architectural tuition, having absorbed the former Edinburgh School of Applied Arts. Classes were conducted at the Royal Institution building on the Mound in central Edinburgh.

Thomson began at the Trustees' School of Art studying within the Architecture section. To some extent the instruction he received would have carried on from his evening classes at Heriot-Watt College, with lessons in perspective and design, drawing from ornament, and preparation of scaled plans.[8] As well as technical drawing ability, Thomson clearly had a strong eye for detail and a methodical approach. He produced many studies of architectural fragments, casts and historical artefacts in the Royal Scottish Museum (now the National Museum of Scotland), including drawings of Persian enamelled friezes, Italian Renaissance stone carving and sixteenth-century armour (Fig. 3, Fig. 4). His skills would have served him well as an architect; a career in the field was within his sights. Before long, though, he was pursuing a new ambition, exploring the possibilities of fine art tuition.

It is not known exactly when Thomson started to supplement his architectural studies with classes in drawing and painting.[9] Seemingly determined to complete his initial course of training, he was allowed to undertake both Diplomas concurrently. By 1907, however, he was firmly established among the fine art students, having attained First Class grades in subjects such as Drawing from

the Antique, Anatomy and Drawing from Life.[10]
A group photograph dating from about 1908 shows
Thomson posing for the camera alongside his
classmates, wearing a painting overall and holding
a palette and brushes (Fig. 5). Some fellow students
have been identified in this image, including
D.M. Sutherland (1883–1973), Eric Robertson
(1887–1941), A.R. Sturrock (1885–1953) and
Walter B. Hislop (1886–1915).[11] Stanley Cursiter
(1887–1976) was also among Thomson's
contemporaries at the Trustees' School of Art.

This was a gifted generation of young artists,
several of whom went on to achieve significant
success. In later life, Thomson was often contacted
by researchers who were eager to learn first-hand
about the student exploits of individuals like Eric
Robertson and Joyce Cary (1888–1957).[12] While
remaining ever discreet, his reminiscences provide
a vivid impression of the times – from descriptions
of tutors and acquaintances, to memories of
impromptu wrestling matches in the Life Class.[13]
The carefree atmosphere recalled by Thomson
is poignant in hindsight, given the traumatic
events that would soon be experienced in the First
World War. The 'old Mound students',[14] as he later
referred to them, were also noteworthy on account
of being the last ones to study there. In 1906 plans
for a new teaching institution were announced,
heralding unprecedented changes to artistic
training in Scotland's capital.

EDINBURGH COLLEGE OF ART
The proposed scheme to create Edinburgh
College of Art was first made public in April 1906,
following the introduction of a parliamentary bill
at Westminster that led to the National Galleries
of Scotland Act (1906).[15] This Act completely
restructured the organisation of the fine arts
in Scotland, with a Board of Trustees for the
National Galleries of Scotland being established
to supersede the outdated Board of Manufactures.
The remit of the new Board did not extend to
art education, and it was decided that teaching
should thus be transferred away from the Mound.

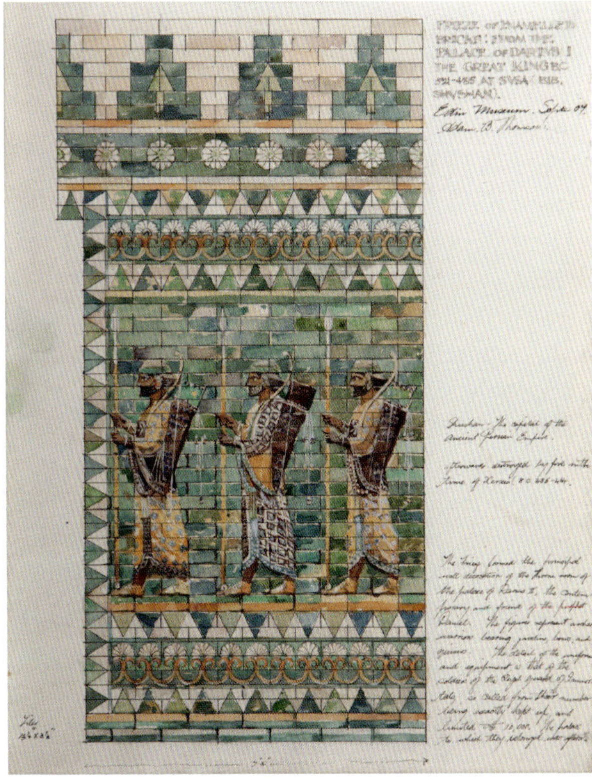

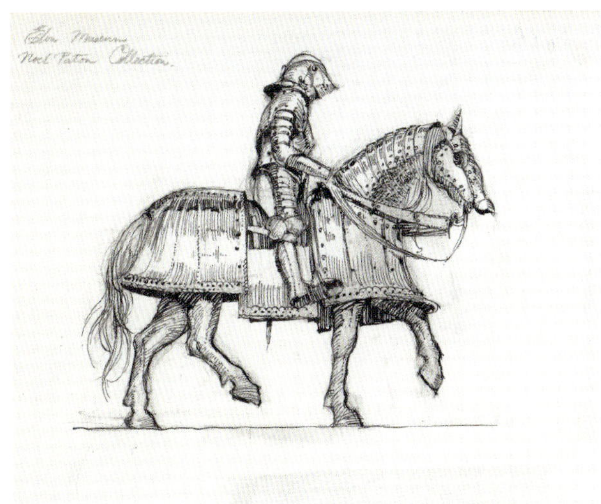

Fig. 3 *(top)* Adam Bruce Thomson, *Frieze of Enamelled Bricks: From the Palace of Darius I, Edinburgh Museum (Study from Cast)*, 1907. Private Collection. © The artist's estate.
(Photograph: The Scottish Gallery)

Fig. 4 *(bottom)* Adam Bruce Thomson, *16th Century Armour, Noel Paton Collection, Edinburgh Museum*, 1906.
Private Collection. © The artist's estate.
(Photograph: Antonia Reeve)

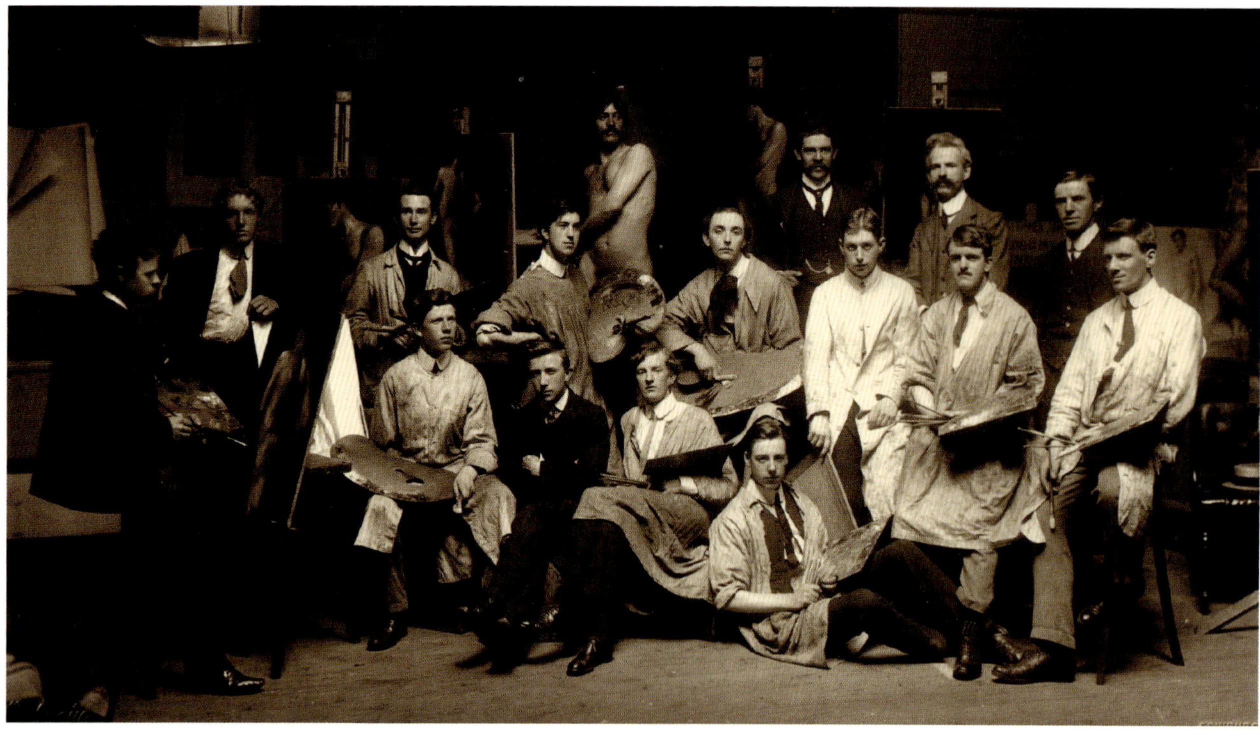

Fig. 5 James C.H. Balmain, *Life Class, Trustees' School of Art, Edinburgh* (Adam Bruce Thomson in middle row, second from left, with easels behind him; see endnote 11 for other people shown), *c.*June 1908. Private Collection.

By way of replacement, a modern facility was proposed to incorporate not only the Trustees' School of Art and its architectural subsidiary, the Edinburgh School of Applied Art, but also the Art Department of Heriot-Watt College and the Royal Scottish Academy Life School. The intention was to dismantle Edinburgh's patchwork of disparate art schools in favour of a more streamlined, municipal institution.[16]

A location for the new College was quickly identified on the site of the old cattle market between Lauriston Place and the Grassmarket, and the foundation stone was laid on 11 July 1907. As construction work commenced, a Board of Management was set up, overseen by the Scottish Education Department and the Town Council. Frank Morley Fletcher (1866–1949) was appointed as the first Director of the College in June 1908, in expectation of it opening that October. Students from the city's existing art schools who had not yet completed their training were allowed to transfer to the new facility. Some tutors also made the transition, with Henry Lintott (1877–1965) and Percy Portsmouth (1874–1953) among those who moved from the Trustees' School of Art.

Adam Bruce Thomson would have been enthusiastic about the prospect. In 1906 he was one of 270 students who had signed a petition drawing attention to the inadequacies of the Royal Institution building, which they deemed too cramped and ill-equipped to accommodate a growing art school.[17] The official prospectus for Edinburgh College of Art promised a much more advanced and comfortable experience. Floor plans showed ample teaching and studio space, with each room naturally lit by windows extending to the ceilings.[18] A modern heating system, easy access to sinks and running water, and a range of new equipment and tools added to the appeal.

In the end, the rapid construction schedule proved too ambitious. The building was not ready for occupation until January 1909, with the result that the first autumn term of teaching had to be conducted within the old setting of the Mound.[19]

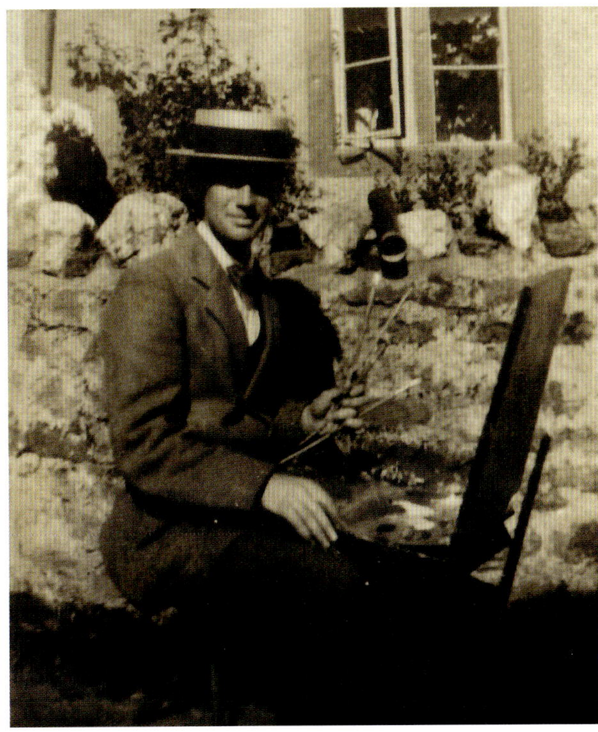

Fig. 6 Unknown Photographer, *Adam Bruce Thomson with Painting Materials*, c.1909–16. Private Collection.

When Thomson was finally able to transfer, he had already completed his Architectural training. He received his Diploma certificate on 7 January 1909. Accordingly, his introduction to the new College and its facilities took place mostly in the Drawing and Painting section, where he was still finishing his second course of studies.

As one of the more advanced students, Thomson joined the College as a 'Student Teacher', a role which involved limited teaching duties and a salary of £25.[20] Stanley Cursiter and Walter B. Hislop, fellow classmates from the Mound, were also employed in this capacity during the 1908–9 session. They found themselves assisting a dynamic department headed by the painter Robert Burns (1869–1941). Under his leadership, established tutors from the Trustees' School of Art were complemented by the progressive approaches of new arrivals like Ernest S. Lumsden (1883–1948) and Mabel Royds (1874–1941). It must have been an inspiring environment. In fact, even before starting at the College, Thomson had already taken the initiative and gained some teaching experience. In the spring of 1908 he worked two days a week as a temporary Art Master at the Royal High School in Edinburgh. A letter of reference from the School's Rector, John Marshall, confirms that he had 'a pleasant quiet manner and seems to earn the respect and liking of his pupils'.[21]

Thomson's abilities as an artist were also starting to attract attention. Towards the end of 1908 he was announced as joint winner of the College's Waterston Prize 'for the best sketch in colours from a subject taken from [George] Borrow's [novel] *Lavengro*'.[22] A few months later, he had his first artwork selected for display at the Royal Scottish Academy (RSA). *A Grey Day* (c.1908) was presented as part of the annual exhibition in January 1909, hung alongside work by artists of national standing. On the point of turning 24 years old, an exciting array of opportunities was opening up before him.

'TRAVELS IN PURSUIT OF THE STUDY OF ART'

During the summer of 1909 Thomson embarked on an extended tour of south-east England. This four-month trip was made possible by a Travelling Scholarship of £40 that he had received from the College with his Architecture Diploma.[23] The purpose was to make a study of British architecture by visiting churches, cathedrals, stately homes and universities. Thomson may no longer have been considering a career as an architect, but he took the project seriously enough, carefully planning his route and itinerary. Hand-drawn maps and diaries suggest that he began in Peterborough and Northampton in July, before moving on to Oxford in August and Cambridge in September. The trip concluded in London in October.[24] Throughout these months, he made numerous drawings of buildings and architectural features, accompanied by historical reference notes. The colleges of Oxford and Cambridge inspired some particularly fine studies (Pl. 2). In London he spent weeks in the South Kensington Museum (now the Victoria and Albert Museum), preparing measured drawings of ironwork and woodcarving. A contemporary sketch by Hanslip Fletcher (1874–1955) shows Thomson hard at work in the museum (Fig. 7).[25]

Thomson returned home at the end of the year, though it would prove to be a short stay. In December 1909 he was presented with his second Diploma – in Drawing and Painting – from the College, followed shortly by another Travelling Scholarship. Of the sixteen Drawing and Painting students who had entered the examinations of the previous session, only three were awarded Diplomas, and only two of those won Travelling Scholarships. Thomson was therefore at the top of his class. His student record reveals that he received a distinction in Anatomy, and passed all other required subjects, including Life Painting, Antique, Composition, Theory of Colour and History of Painting.[26]

For his second Travelling Scholarship, Thomson was awarded £60, a sum which enabled a more ambitious programme of study. He determined to journey through France and Spain, visiting galleries and exploring the local sights. The trip began in London in January 1910. Diary entries show that he spent about three weeks there, viewing artworks in the National Gallery and Wallace Collection.[27] Old Master paintings by Tintoretto, Velázquez and Rembrandt impressed him enough to make notes on their composition and colour palette. He also enjoyed walks along the Thames, sketching the bridges and boats around Lambeth and Chelsea at different times of day. While in London, he socialised with fellow Edinburgh graduates Eric Robertson and Wilma Law Weir.

In mid-February Thomson moved on to Paris, where Walter B. Hislop's brother Gordon helped him find lodgings at 9 Rue de Sommerard in the Latin Quarter. Contemporary writings suggest that he regarded the trip as something of an adventure; his diary bears the subheading 'Travels in Pursuit of the Study of Art'. The Louvre was one of the main attractions on Thomson's itinerary, and he dedicated himself to examining and copying

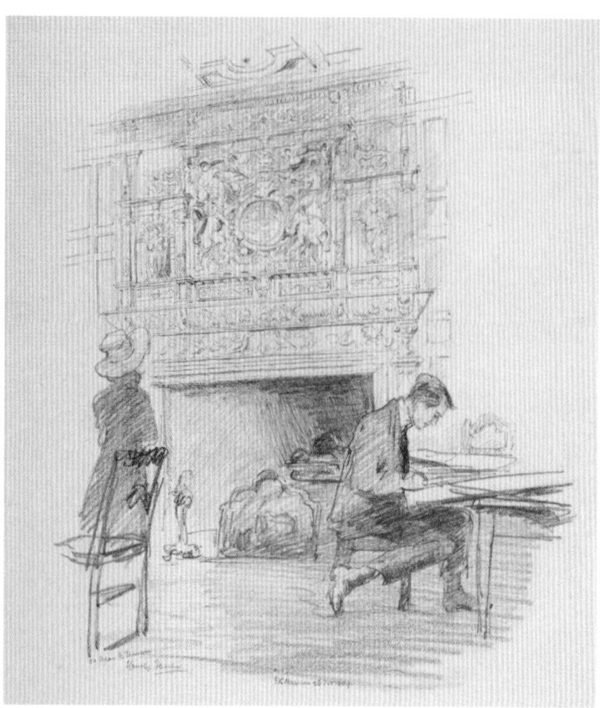

Fig. 7 Hanslip Fletcher, *Adam Bruce Thomson in South Kensington Museum*, 1909. Private Collection. © The artist's estate. (Photograph: The Scottish Gallery)

artworks in its collection. The practice of copying from the Old Masters was an integral aspect of art education at the time, intended to help students gain a deeper understanding of painterly techniques and processes. Thomson would have learned copying skills in Edinburgh and was expected to return with a portfolio of work.

Notre Dame Cathedral was another highlight (Fig. 8). The young artist was immediately struck by this building, describing it as 'a magnificent Cathedral full of height and mysterious light'.[28] He visited almost every day to sketch its interior and architectural details. Thomson was able to share these experiences with friends. As in London, he met up again with Eric Robertson, who was travelling with the artist John Duncan (1866–1945). Duncan accompanied them to several galleries, as well as providing an invitation to the studio of J.D. Fergusson (1874–1961), who had settled in Paris in 1907. Thomson later recalled that Fergusson introduced him to the avant-garde paintings of Henri Matisse.[29]

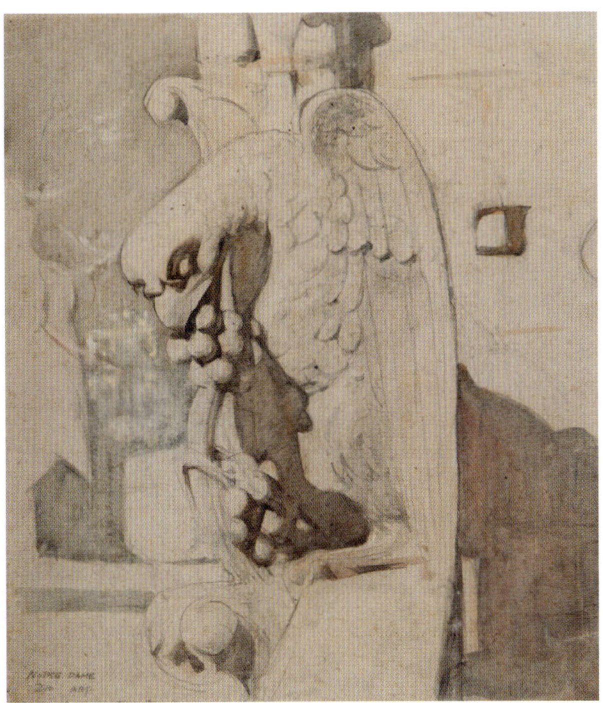

Fig. 8 Adam Bruce Thomson, *Notre Dame*, 1910.
Private Collection. © The artist's estate.
(Photograph: The Scottish Gallery)

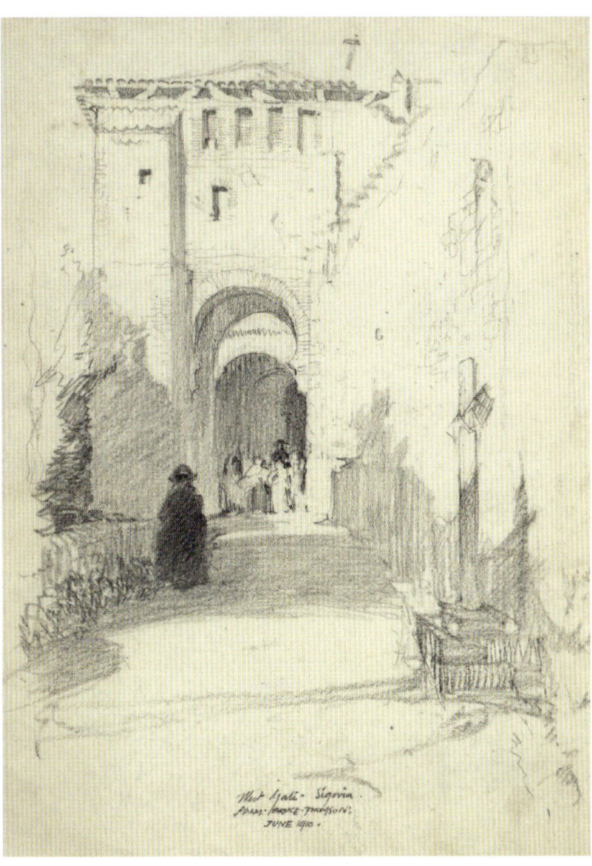

Fig. 9 Adam Bruce Thomson, *West Gate, Segovia*, 1910.
Private Collection. © The artist's estate.
(Photograph: Antonia Reeve)

After two months in the French capital, Thomson journeyed south to Spain, arriving in Burgos on 13 April 1910. He spoke 'not a word of Spanish' and initially felt out of his depth, but was soon befriended by the Dutch artist Frits Lensvelt (1886–1945), with whom he 'hit it off'.[30] The pair travelled together to Ávila, where Thomson sketched local buildings and carthorses. Towards the end of April, he relocated to Madrid. He found the city itself disappointing, though its rich art collections were a consolation. As he noted in his diary: 'No churches, no river, no picturesque buildings, nothing but the Prado.'[31] In the Prado Museum he concentrated on paintings by Velázquez, making copies of masterpieces like *Las Meninas* (1656). Madrid also provided a convenient base to explore other towns. Between early May and late June, he visited Toledo and Segovia, which he appreciated for their colour, light and scenery. These locations inspired a number of accomplished drawings and paintings, and at least one related etching (Fig. 9).[32]

By July 1910 Thomson was on his way back to Scotland. He stopped off briefly in Paris and Rouen, before continuing on to London. The British Museum was among his final destinations, where he saw etchings by Rembrandt and Whistler. The evocative landscapes of the latter, described by Thomson as 'charming […] very simple and reserved', made a lasting impression.[33]

A BURGEONING CAREER

Upon Thomson's return home, he was appointed to the staff of Edinburgh College of Art. He began the 1910–11 session as an Assistant Teacher in the Drawing and Painting section, working ten hours a week. Within a year his duties had been extended to cover twenty hours a week, taking both daytime and evening classes.[34] He was now teaching alongside former tutors, and would

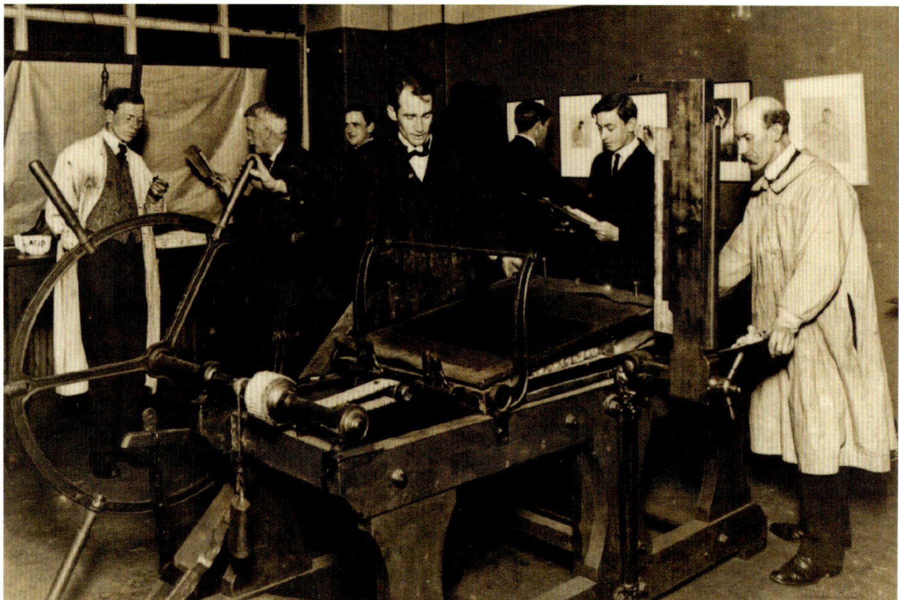

Fig. 10 Unknown Photographer, *Adam Bruce Thomson with Printing Press, Edinburgh College of Art*, *c.*1909–16. Private Collection.

soon be joined by his friends Walter B. Hislop and D.M. Sutherland, who became members of staff in 1912. Thomson taught a range of subjects at the College, including elementary drawing and colour theory. The student roll was increasing, and it appears that tutors were in high demand – for the 1912–13 session he had to request that his evening teaching hours be reduced.[35]

Like most of his colleagues, Thomson balanced classroom commitments with the development of his own artistic practice. At this stage, his main interest was printmaking. The College boasted state-of-the-art printmaking facilities, which were open to staff and students (Fig. 10). As the 1908–9 Annual Report explains:

> A studio was set apart and equipped with a press and the apparatus necessary for Etching and Aquatint work. The opportunity provided for this work and the teaching that was given attracted a small group of advanced students and practising artists, who, during the Session carried out original work.[36]

Thomson's early etchings demonstrate both his consummate draughtsmanship and his growing confidence with printmaking techniques. Some,

such as *Craigleith Quarry* (*c.*1907–9, Fig. 11) and *Edinburgh – Canal Basin* (*c.*1913, Fig. 12, Pl. 6), depict industrial subjects and city views. Others portray rural scenes of farm buildings, trees and open countryside. These locations are often difficult to identify. Indeed, almost all of the artist's etchings are undated, which makes it hard to chart his progress in the medium.[37] Records show that his first ever exhibit at the Royal Glasgow Institute of the Fine Arts (RGI) was an etching entitled *Edinburgh from South*, which was displayed in 1913.[38] In 1915 he submitted another two etchings to the RGI annual exhibition, *Edinburgh, from Murrayfield* and *Suggested by Caerlaverock Castle*, the former of which he had shown the previous year at the Society of Scottish Artists (SSA).[39]

During this period, Thomson also experimented with lithography. He seems to have reserved this technique mostly for portraiture, attempting to recapture the spontaneity of sketching in pencil. A series of sensitive head-and-shoulder studies present young women in fashionable attire (Fig. 13). These may have been undertaken as portrait commissions, but they are perhaps more likely to have been informal exercises, in which Thomson recorded impressions of friends and

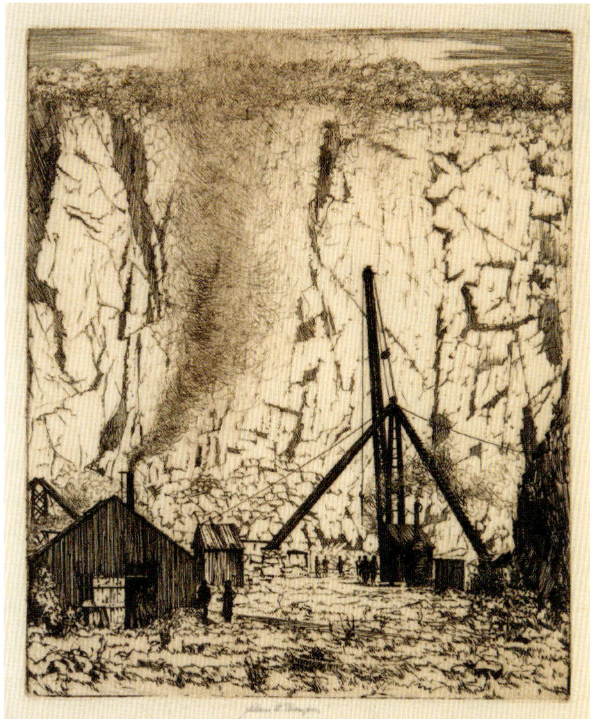

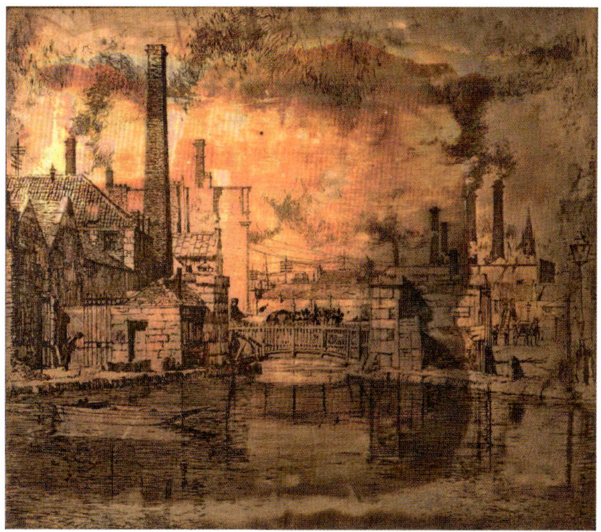

Fig. 11 *(top)* Adam Bruce Thomson, *Craigleith Quarry*, *c*.1907–9. Royal Scottish Academy. Purchased 2020, with 50% grant from National Fund for Acquisitions. © The artist's estate. (Photograph: Royal Scottish Academy)

Fig. 12 *(bottom)* Adam Bruce Thomson, copper etching plate for *Edinburgh – Canal Basin*, *c*.1913. City Art Centre, City of Edinburgh Museums and Galleries. © The artist's estate. (Photograph: Antonia Reeve)

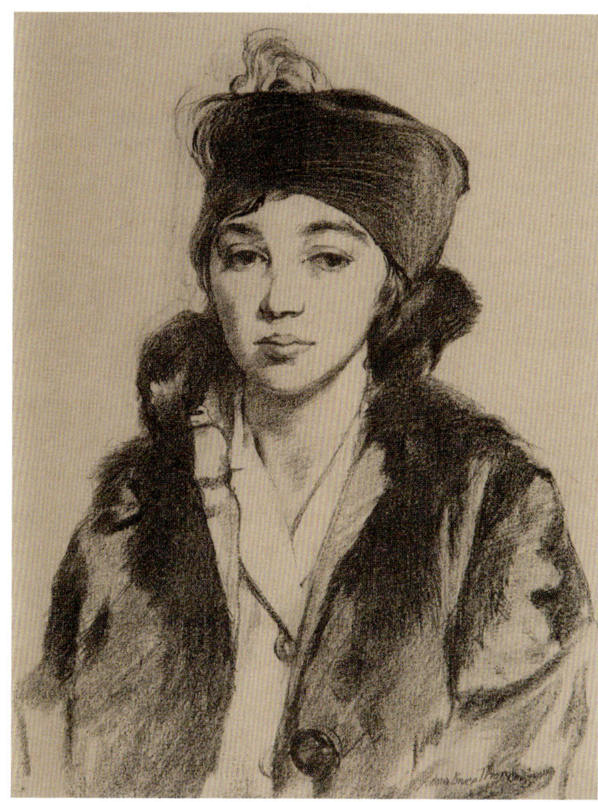

Fig. 13 Adam Bruce Thomson, *Miss Chambers*, *c*.1910–15. Private Collection. © The artist's estate. (Photograph: The Scottish Gallery)

acquaintances with the intention of translating them into lithographs. Only a few of these works identify the sitters. The artist did, however, use the same technique to make at least one self-portrait (Pl.1).

According to contemporary notes, Thomson found practical instruction on lithography in the writings of Hubert von Herkomer (1849–1914).[40] He sought further advice from experienced local artists, including James Cadenhead (1858–1927), David Alison (1882–1955) and the Principal of Edinburgh College of Art, Frank Morley Fletcher, who was a great champion of printmaking as a fine art discipline. Thomson recorded his discoveries as he gradually mastered the lithographic process, noting his satisfaction when he achieved the desired results. *Girls Sketching* (1915, Pl. 7) was among the efforts he analysed, commenting on the

'Difficulty in bringing up shadow on Carola's face – is better not so dark as first print.' This composition is now one of his best-known lithographs; a copy is held by the National Galleries of Scotland.

WAR

Between 1911 and 1914 Thomson continued to find inspiration travelling away from home. In September 1911 he toured Orkney, visiting Kirkwall and Stromness, and drawing prehistoric standing stones at the Ring of Brodgar.[41] In the same year he also journeyed to the Netherlands, accompanied by Walter B. Hislop. He spent several holidays exploring the landscapes of Dumfries and Galloway, and made at least one return trip to London in 1913. Each expedition proved fruitful, affording opportunities for mental rejuvenation and sketching. Such freedoms came to a sudden halt in 1914, however, with the outbreak of the First World War.

The impact of the conflict was felt quickly at Edinburgh College of Art. Within days of the autumn term commencing, it was reported that several members of staff from the Drawing and Painting section had left their teaching posts to undertake military service.[42] These included Thomson's close friend Walter B. Hislop, who joined the 5th Battalion of the Royal Scots Regiment. Those who remained faced considerable extra work to cover the remits of their absent colleagues. A small number of new teachers were appointed to fill vacancies, such as the talented recent graduate Dorothy Johnstone (1892–1980). On the whole, however, staffing capacity at the College was stretched.

Thomson carried on his teaching duties, instructing classes in the Architecture section as well as Drawing and Painting. He also took charge of Etching tuition when Thomas Duncan Rhind (1871–1927) departed for the army, initially doing so without any additional payment.[43] Throughout these months, Thomson continued to develop his own practice, focusing on landscape scenes and portraiture. From around 1914 onwards he had

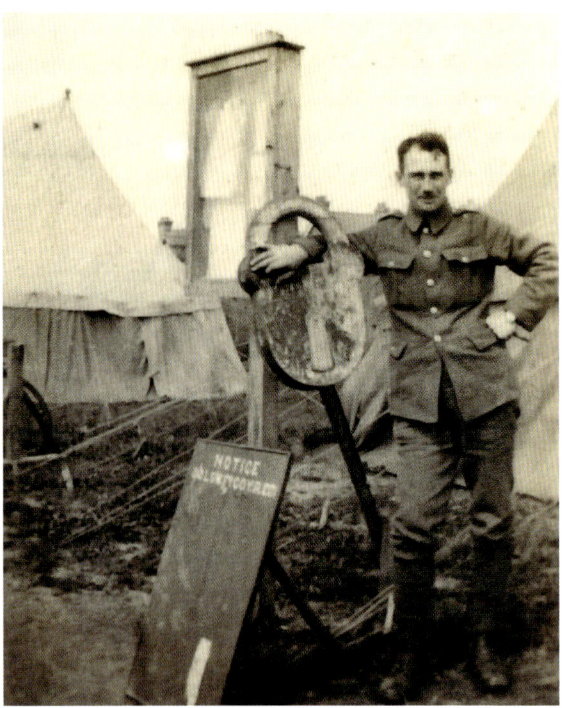

Fig. 14 Unknown Photographer, *Adam Bruce Thomson during Military Service*, 1916–18. Private Collection.

use of studio space at the old Synod Hall on Castle Terrace. He maintained regular contributions to the exhibitions of the Royal Scottish Academy and other artist-led societies, ensuring that his work had a consistent public platform.[44]

These professional endeavours were pursued against a backdrop of increasing uncertainty and personal strain. Growing numbers of friends and colleagues were involved in fighting on different fronts. In June 1915 the College's Board of Management recorded that Walter B. Hislop had been reported missing in action. His family later learned that he had been killed on 28 April while serving in the Gallipoli campaign. The news was a painful blow.[45]

In late 1915 Thomson voluntarily enlisted for military service under the Derby Scheme. He was called up in February 1916, joining the Royal Engineers a few weeks later (Fig. 14). Initially, he was posted to Witham in Essex, where he was engaged in training exercises building bridges and laying roads. In his diary, Thomson remarked that the outdoor manual work was hard, but that

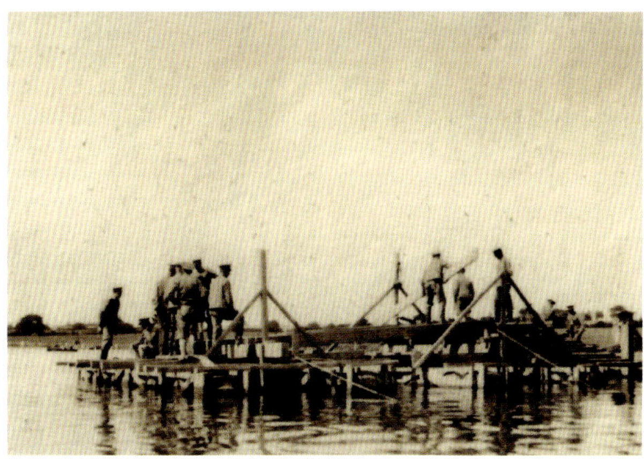

Fig. 15 *(above)* Adam Bruce Thomson, *Royal Engineers Building a Bridge*, 1916–18. Private Collection.

Fig. 16 *(right)* Adam Bruce Thomson, *Royal Engineers Building a Suspension Bridge*, 1916–18. Private Collection.

he 'learned a great deal'.[46] He was subsequently promoted to the rank of Second Lieutenant. Despite the circumstances, there was still time for sketching. Whilst stationed in Witham, he witnessed the aftermath of a German Zeppelin crash-landing into nearby farmland and made a detailed drawing of the scene, which was later reproduced as a postcard (Pl. 9).

As the war progressed, Thomson served in France and Belgium. Between 1917 and 1918 the Royal Engineers played a key role in the Allies' advance, repairing damaged road and rail links and constructing bridges over waterways (Fig. 15, Fig. 16). Much of their work was conducted under threat of shelling and gas attacks. Thomson spent time in Arras, and was billeted near Mons when the Armistice was declared in November 1918.

Like many of his generation, he spoke little of his wartime experiences afterwards. He was nonetheless profoundly affected by them. Decades later he described visiting the grave of Walter B. Hislop's brother John at Aubigny-en-Artois while on his way to be demobilised. The desolate sight was imprinted on his memory: 'The melancholy, utterly sad landscape, the blasted trees, the muddy ground reflecting the last of the winter's day twilight and in the cemetery the rows and rows of our chaps.'[47]

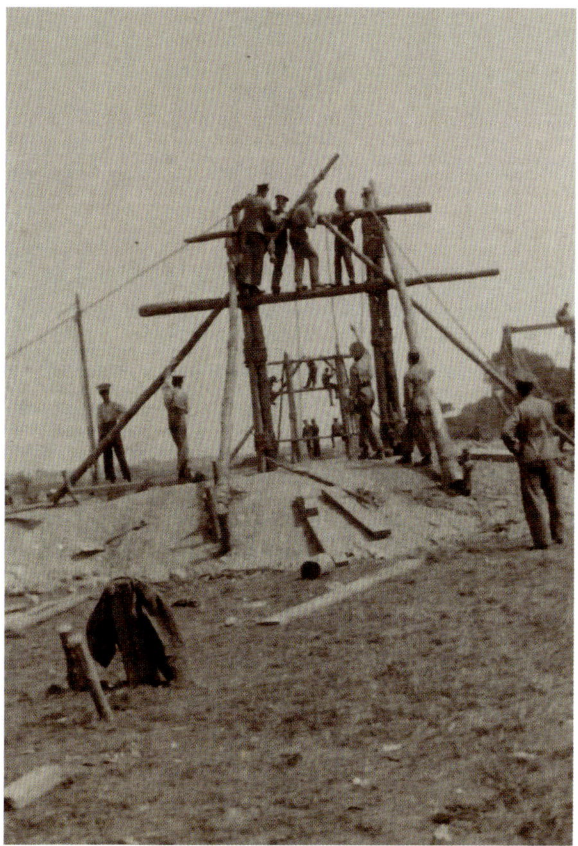

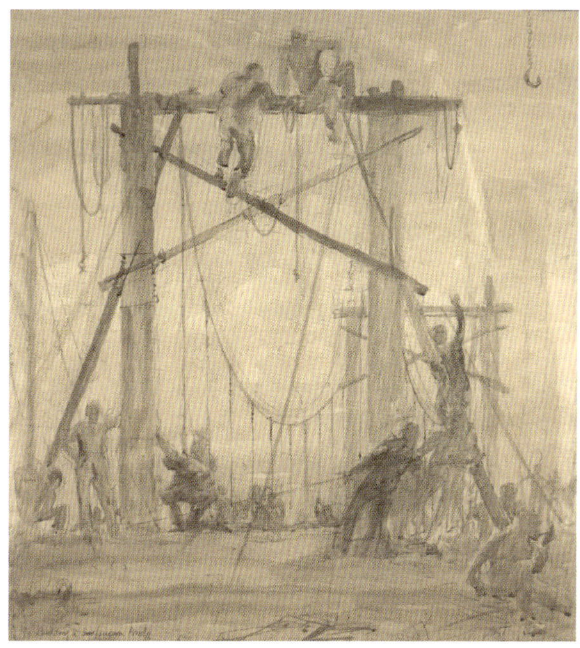

Fig. 17 Adam Bruce Thomson, *Royal Engineers Building a Suspension Bridge*, c.1916. Private Collection.
© The artist's estate. (Photograph: Antonia Reeve)

Thomson made a series of ink and wash drawings based on his time with the Royal Engineers. Many of them depict soldiers labouring on the construction of suspension bridges and pontoons (Fig. 17). These studies were most likely produced away from the front line, either during training exercises or periods of leave. They may even have been created after the war. Related lithographs, such as *Royal Engineers Building a Bridge near Mons* (1918, Pl. 10), were certainly printed at a later date. According to family and friends, Thomson had an impressive facility for sketching from memory. He also appears to have used photographs as source material. In one surviving album there are several wartime photographs taken by Thomson which bear a close resemblance to his suspension bridge compositions. The considered pictorial arrangement of these drawings suggests the benefit of hindsight. The repeated use of silhouettes as a dramatic device similarly indicates that the artist was interpreting his experiences gradually, working towards an increasingly simplified, elegiac style. Wartime subjects were an extended preoccupation. He continued to exhibit such scenes at the RSA until 1923.

HOMECOMING

For Thomson, the war years brought loss and sorrow, but also hope for the future. On 15 April 1918 he married Jessie Inglis Hislop, the sister of his late friend Walter B. Hislop (Fig. 18). The couple had known each other for some years. In October 1915 Thomson made a lithographic portrait of Jessie, and the following year John Hislop wrote to him mentioning their relationship. In the letter, John refers affectionately to his sister as 'the wee red-haired lassie', though he warns his future brother-in-law that 'she does not approve of the term "red"!!!'.[48] Jessie became the artist's lifelong partner, a source of steadfast support and companionship.

After the war, the newlyweds set up home at 149 Warrender Park Road, a tenement in

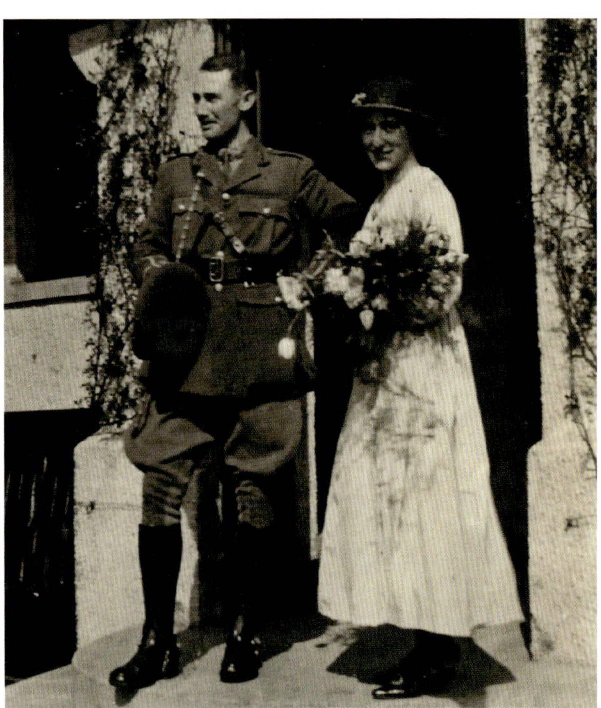

Fig. 18 Unknown Photographer, *Adam Bruce Thomson and Jessie Inglis Hislop on Their Wedding Day, Edinburgh*, 15 April 1918. Private Collection.

the Marchmont area of Edinburgh. A previous occupant, the painter Duncan Cameron (1837–1916), had installed a purpose-built studio on the top floor of the building when it was constructed in the 1880s.[49] With north-facing windows and skylights, and close proximity to Bruntsfield Links, it was an ideal setting for Thomson to resume his career and start a family.

The couple's first child, Ronald, was born in November 1919. A daughter, Margaret, arrived in 1921, followed by Mary in 1924. Thomson was deeply attached to his wife and children, and often depicted them in his work. He made scores of rapid portrait sketches throughout the 1920s, capturing different stages of childhood as the family grew. He also produced more detailed compositions. The pastel drawing *Young Family* (c.1920–25, Pl. 11) provides an early example – a carefully observed study of Jessie resting with a baby outdoors. The interplay of sunlight and shadow across the two figures adds a particular tenderness to this peaceful scene.

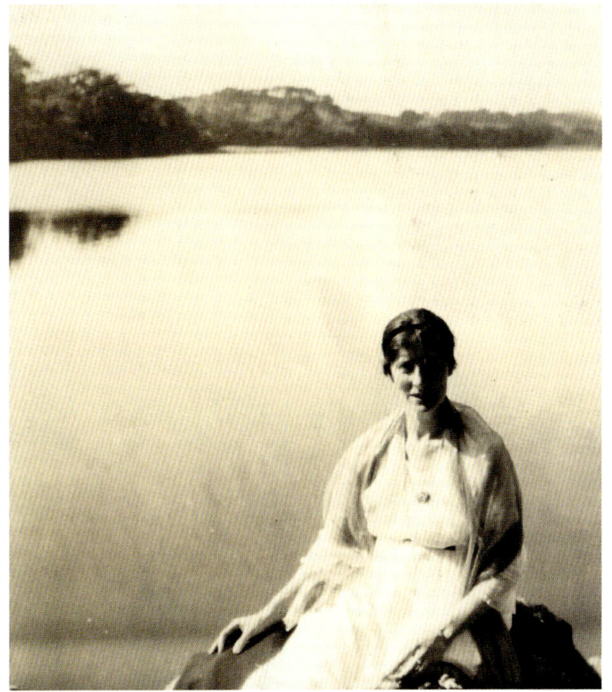

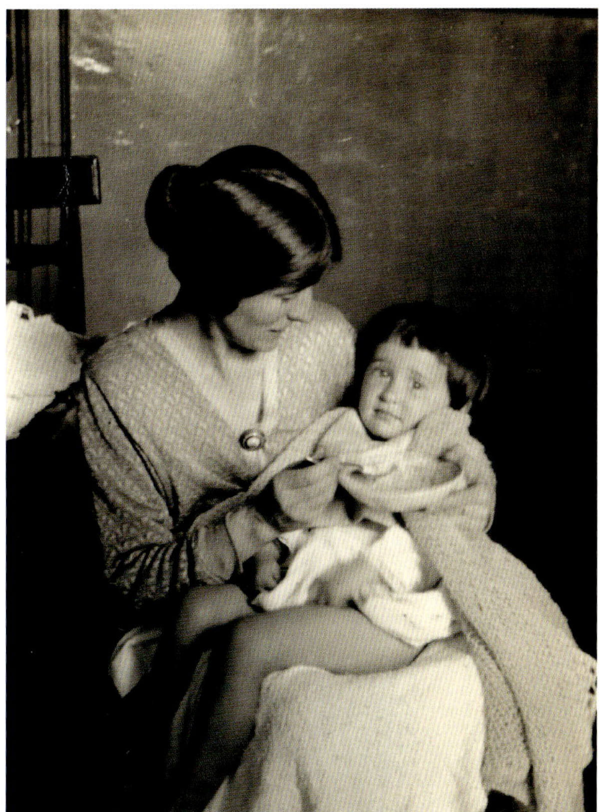

Pastels became an important medium over the next few years. As well as portraits, Thomson used them in small-scale landscapes and rural views (Fig. 22, Fig. 23). The jewel-like colours offered an arresting visual contrast to his monochrome work as a printmaker. Pastels were also appealing on a practical level. They could easily be carried and deployed away from the studio, allowing the artist to respond more immediately to external stimuli. Executed on tinted paper, Thomson's pastel drawings have an exceptional fluency and directness of touch. His aptitude caught the attention of contemporary critics. In 1927 an article in *The Studio* noted that his 'experimental exploits with pastels' had led to 'some distinctly captivating and intrinsically artistic results'.[50]

Thomson exhibited and sold pastel drawings alongside etchings and paintings. His return to oil painting after the war seems to have been somewhat tentative, and for the first few years his main output was works on paper. When he did eventually resume his practice in oils he found inspiration in landscapes, but also domestic subjects.

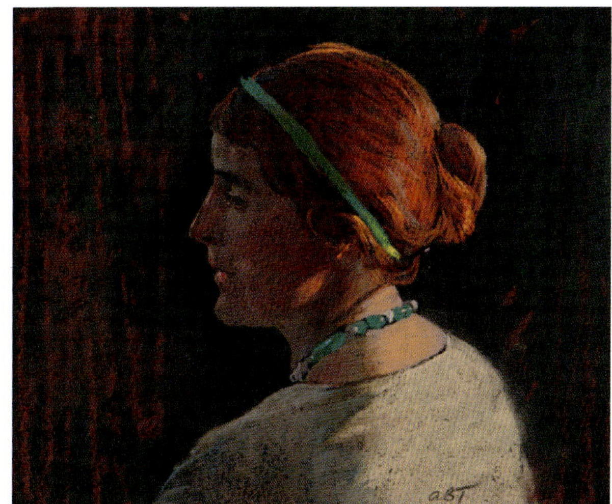

Fig. 19 *(top)* Adam Bruce Thomson, *Jessie*, September 1922. Private Collection.

Fig. 20 *(bottom)* Adam Bruce Thomson, *Jessie with Mary*, mid-1920s. Private Collection.

Fig. 21 Adam Bruce Thomson, *Jessie*, c.1922. Private Collection. © The artist's estate. (Photograph: The Scottish Gallery)

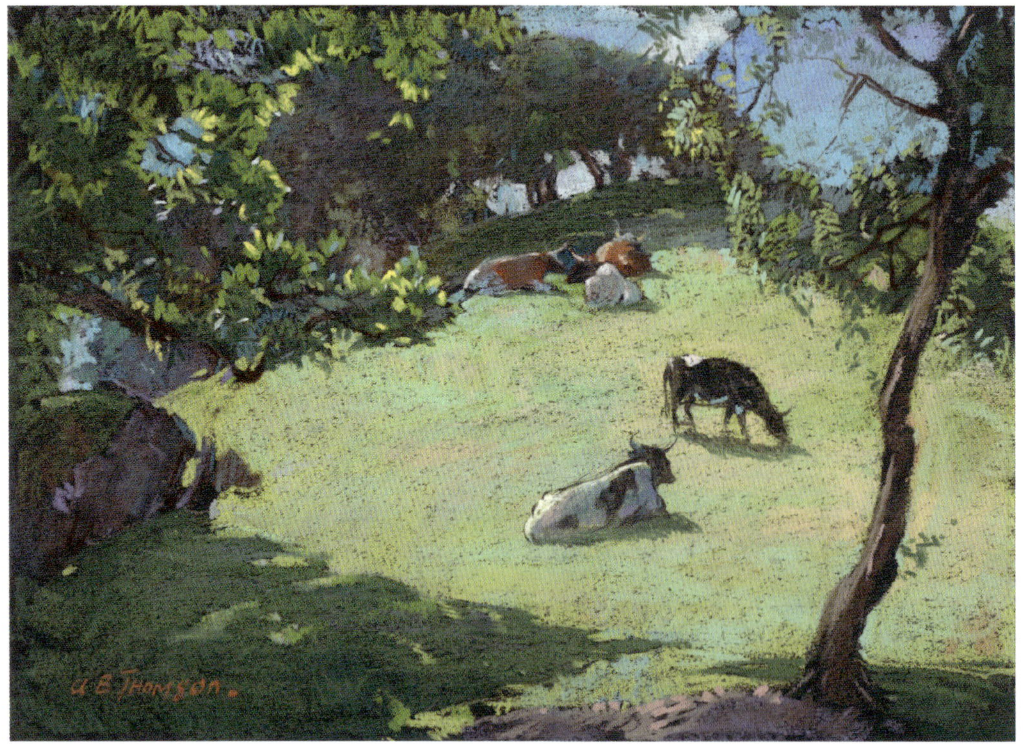

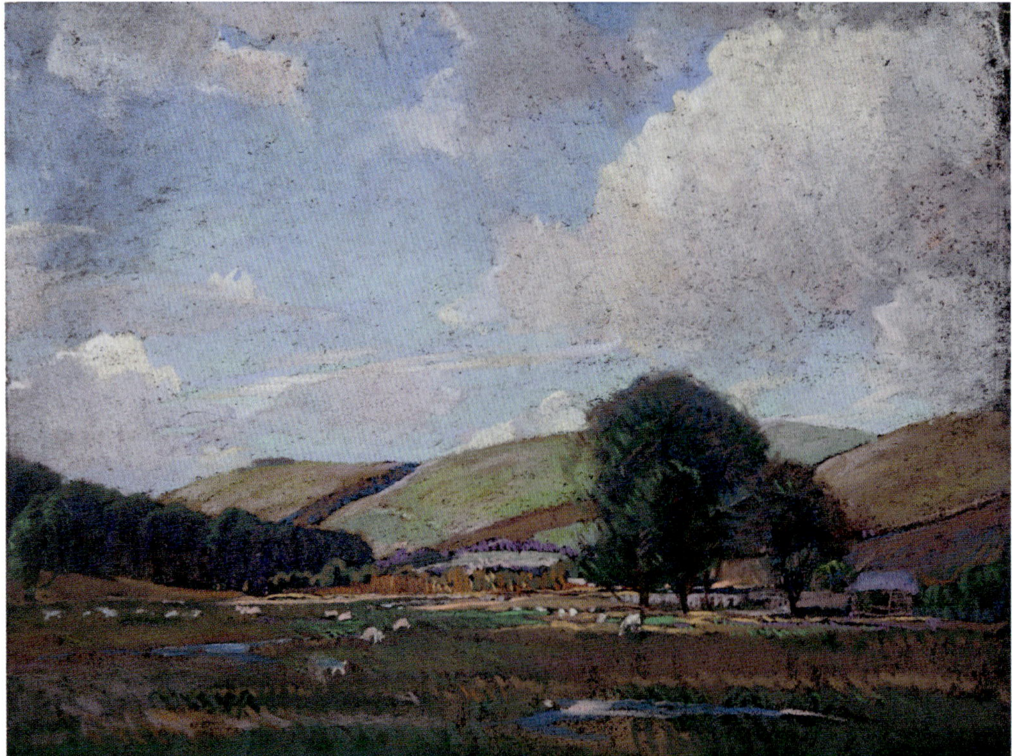

Fig. 22 *(top)* Adam Bruce Thomson, *Trees and Cattle, Colvend*, 1920s. City Art Centre, City of Edinburgh Museums and Galleries. © The artist's estate. (Photograph: Antonia Reeve)

Fig. 23 *(bottom)* Adam Bruce Thomson, *Primside Mill*, 1920s. Private Collection. © The artist's estate. (Photograph: The Scottish Gallery)

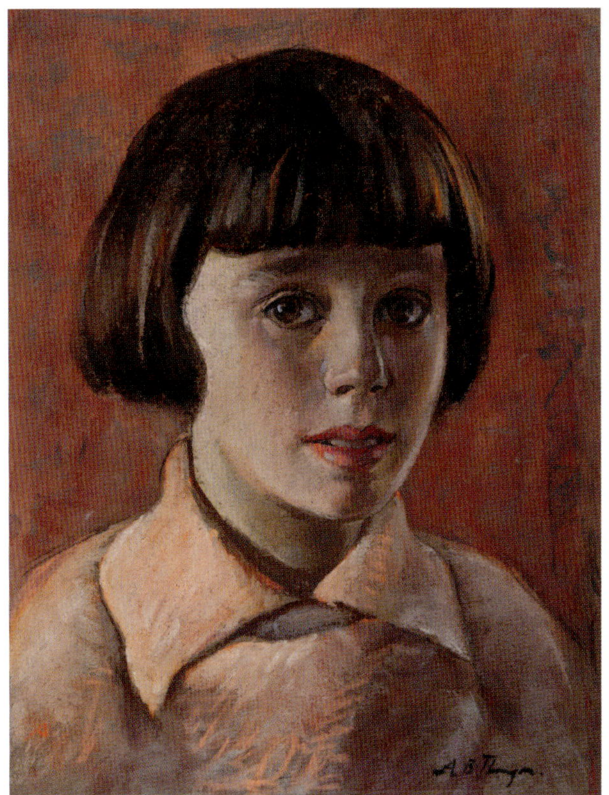

Fig. 24 Adam Bruce Thomson, *Margaret*, late 1920s.
Private Collection. © The artist's estate.
(Photograph: The Scottish Gallery)

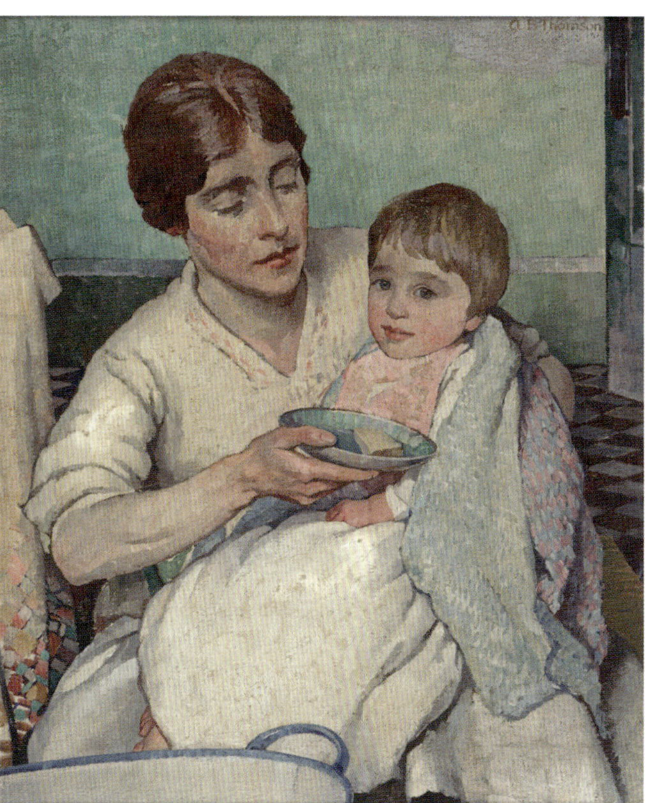

Fig. 25 Adam Bruce Thomson, *Mother and Child*, c.1927.
Private Collection. © The artist's estate.
(Photograph: Antonia Reeve)

The 1920s saw him complete a number of
notable still-life and interior scenes. These works
were painted on a gesso ground and have a
dry, matte appearance. The colour palette is
predominantly pale, giving the impression of weak
daylight entering the room. In several instances
objects are presented against the backdrop of a
window, through which the outside world awaits.
From My Bedroom Window (mid-1920s, Pl. 13)
was one of Thomson's most successful efforts in
this genre. Having garnered critical praise at the
1929 Royal Scottish Academy annual exhibition,
the canvas was purchased for the nation by the
Scottish Modern Arts Association.[51] In later decades
the artist continued to explore still-life themes,
though the complex compositional structures of his
early works gradually gave way to more simple,
naturalistic depictions of flowers gathered in
vases (Pl. 27).

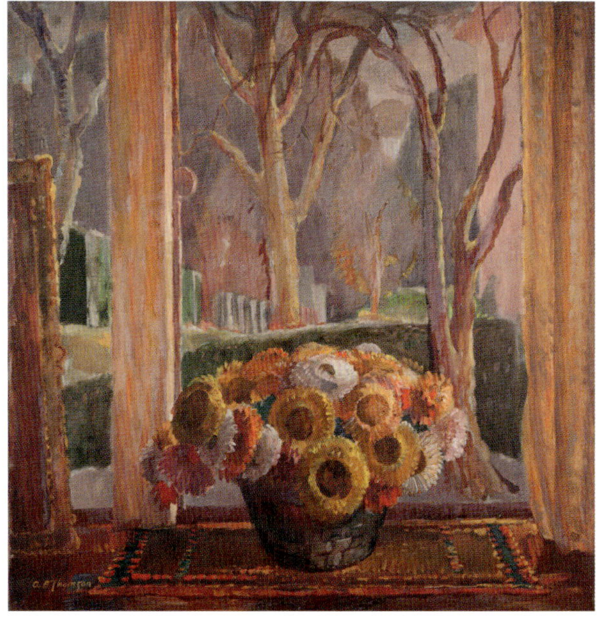

Fig. 26 Adam Bruce Thomson, *Immortelles at the Window*, c.1930.
Private Collection. © The artist's estate.
(Photograph: The Scottish Gallery)

A RETURN TO TEACHING

The end of the war also allowed Thomson to recommence his teaching career. Edinburgh College of Art had been considerably scarred by four years of conflict. By 1918 at least 91 staff and students were known to have died.[52] Thomson returned to teaching duties in February 1919, and was soon instructing classes in a range of subjects. Meetings of the Board of Management record that during the 1919–20 session he taught Colour Theory, Still Life Painting, Etching and a Preparatory Life Class for women.[53] Student numbers swelled as many whose tuition had been interrupted by the war came back to complete their training. Readjusting to civilian life must have been difficult for tutors and students alike, but shared experiences meant that survivors often formed close bonds. In 1919 David Alison succeeded Robert Burns as Head of Drawing and Painting. He restructured the department, populating it with younger tutors such as Penelope Beaton (1886–1963) and Donald Moodie (1892–1963).

Throughout the 1920s Thomson played an especially impactful role as Teacher of Etching. These classes were supplementary to the main curriculum and were conducted in the evenings, operating almost as a club. They were extremely well attended. In 1925 the College considered increasing the number of classes from two evenings per week to three, such was demand for enrolment.[54] Thomson was respected for his knowledge and skills as a printmaker, though his popularity also stemmed from his tutoring style. Patient and constructive, he spurred on the next generation of artist-printmakers, taking a significant hand in the development of figures like William Crozier (1893–1930) and William Wilson (1905–1972). Thomson spotted Wilson's potential while the teenager was attending evening classes on a part-time basis, encouraging him to take up full-time training. He is also credited with introducing Wilson to Ian Fleming (1906–1994), a Glasgow School of Art graduate who went on to become another acclaimed printmaker in the 1930s. Much esteemed as a mentor, Thomson enjoyed lifelong friendships with many of his students.[55]

EDINBURGH – ENERGY AND INSPIRATION

This period marked the beginning of the revival of Edinburgh's artistic scene. Over the next twenty years the city would become home to a thriving community with a distinctly progressive agenda. Thomson's position on the staff at Edinburgh College of Art placed him at the heart of these developments. His connections were further strengthened through regular involvement with artist-led exhibiting societies. Engaged and informed, he would have felt the changes in the air.

For many Scottish artists, the 1920s and 1930s was the era when Modernist influences from the Continent finally took hold. Trailblazing individuals like J.D. Fergusson and S.J. Peploe (1871–1935) reached their maturity responding to avant-garde innovations in France. Meanwhile, younger figures such as William Gillies, John Maxwell and William Johnstone (1897–1981), who had benefited from travelling scholarships to Paris in the aftermath of the First World War, returned home with new ideas and attitudes. Fauvism, Cubism and abstraction transformed ways of

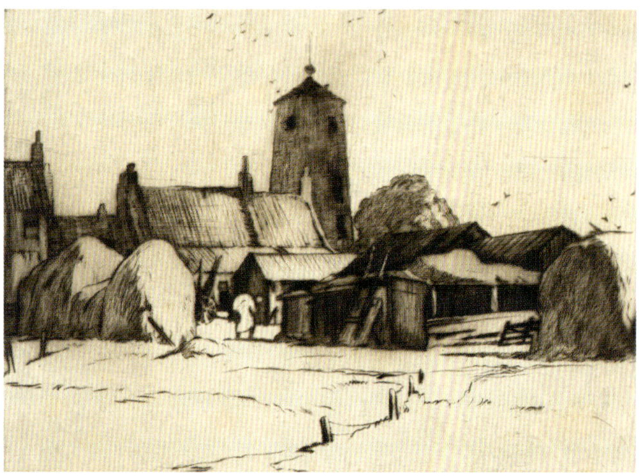

Fig. 27 Adam Bruce Thomson, *The Mill, Norham*, *c*.1926. Private Collection. © The artist's estate.
(Photograph: Antonia Reeve)

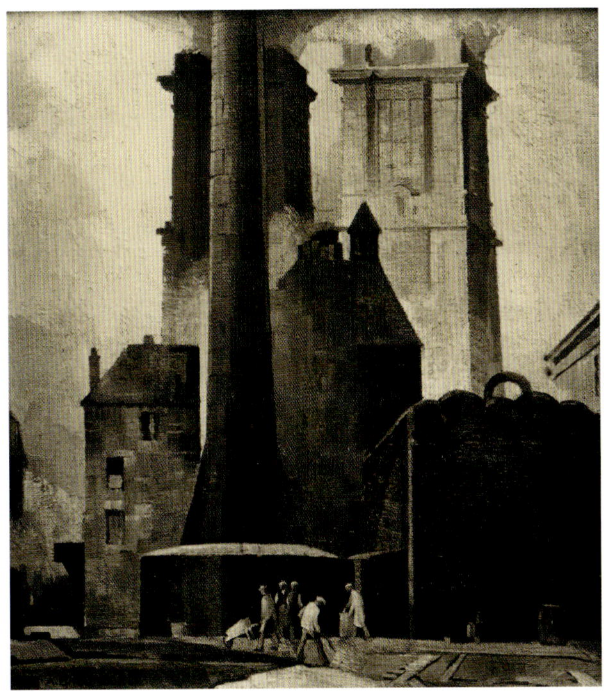

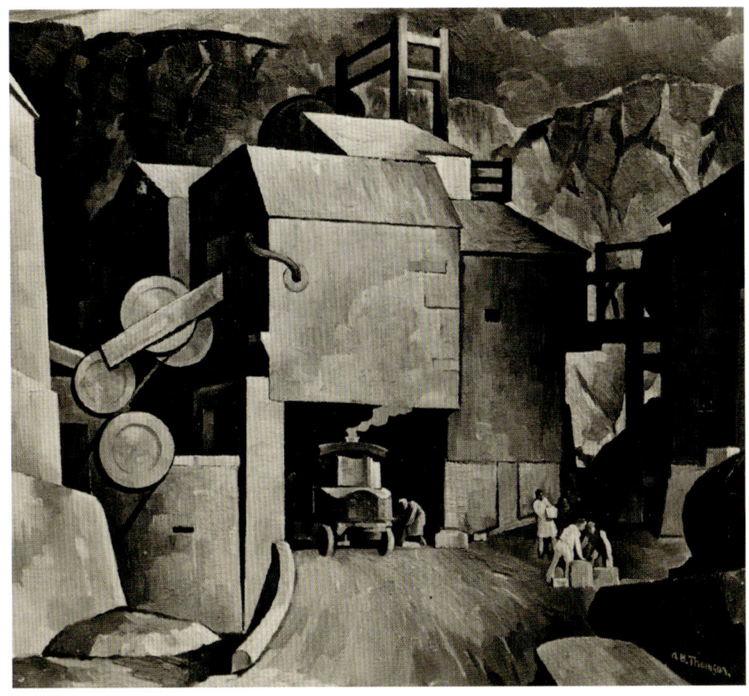

Fig. 28 Adam Bruce Thomson, *The Cooling Towers* (black and white reproduction), *c.*1926. Untraced. © The artist's estate.

Fig. 29 Adam Bruce Thomson, *The Stone Crushers* (black and white reproduction), *c.*1929. Untraced. © The artist's estate.

understanding and creating art, casting aside more traditional modes of representation. Colour, form and mood became the prevailing concerns.[56] This trend was fuelled not only by greater opportunities to travel, but also by increased access to displays of international modern art. In Edinburgh, the Society of Scottish Artists did much in this regard, showcasing pieces by Pablo Picasso, Amedeo Modigliani and Henri Matisse in its annual exhibitions, as well as staging major displays of work by Edvard Munch and Paul Klee.[57]

Although Thomson was older than many of his peers in the Modernist vanguard, he was not immune to the shift. In the mid-1920s he began experimenting with a Cubist style of painting, simplifying forms into flat planes of colour and enhancing geometric outlines. A flavour of this approach is evident in the crisp architecture of *New Galloway* (*c.*1922–5, Pl. 15). However, the phase reached its fullest culmination in *The Cooling Towers* (*c.*1926, Fig. 28) and *The Stone Crushers* (*c.*1929, Fig. 29). These two paintings are currently untraced, though surviving black and white photographs of them are revealing. They show Thomson absorbing and reinterpreting the formal vocabulary of Cubism in a manner similar to his friend and former student William Crozier. In particular, it is worth noting his use of strong tonal contrasts to heighten the drama of each scene. The same device was employed by Crozier in his brooding cityscape *Edinburgh (from Salisbury Crags)* (*c.*1927). Previous art historical research has claimed that Thomson's paintings of the 1930s were inspired by Crozier's example,[58] but these earlier experiments suggest a more nuanced dialogue between the pair. Indeed, a contemporary review of the 1929 Society of Scottish Artists annual exhibition named both artists as contributing 'some of the more interesting works' in the show.[59]

Crozier's premature death in December 1930 was a shock to the tight-knit artistic community. Afterwards, Thomson grew ever

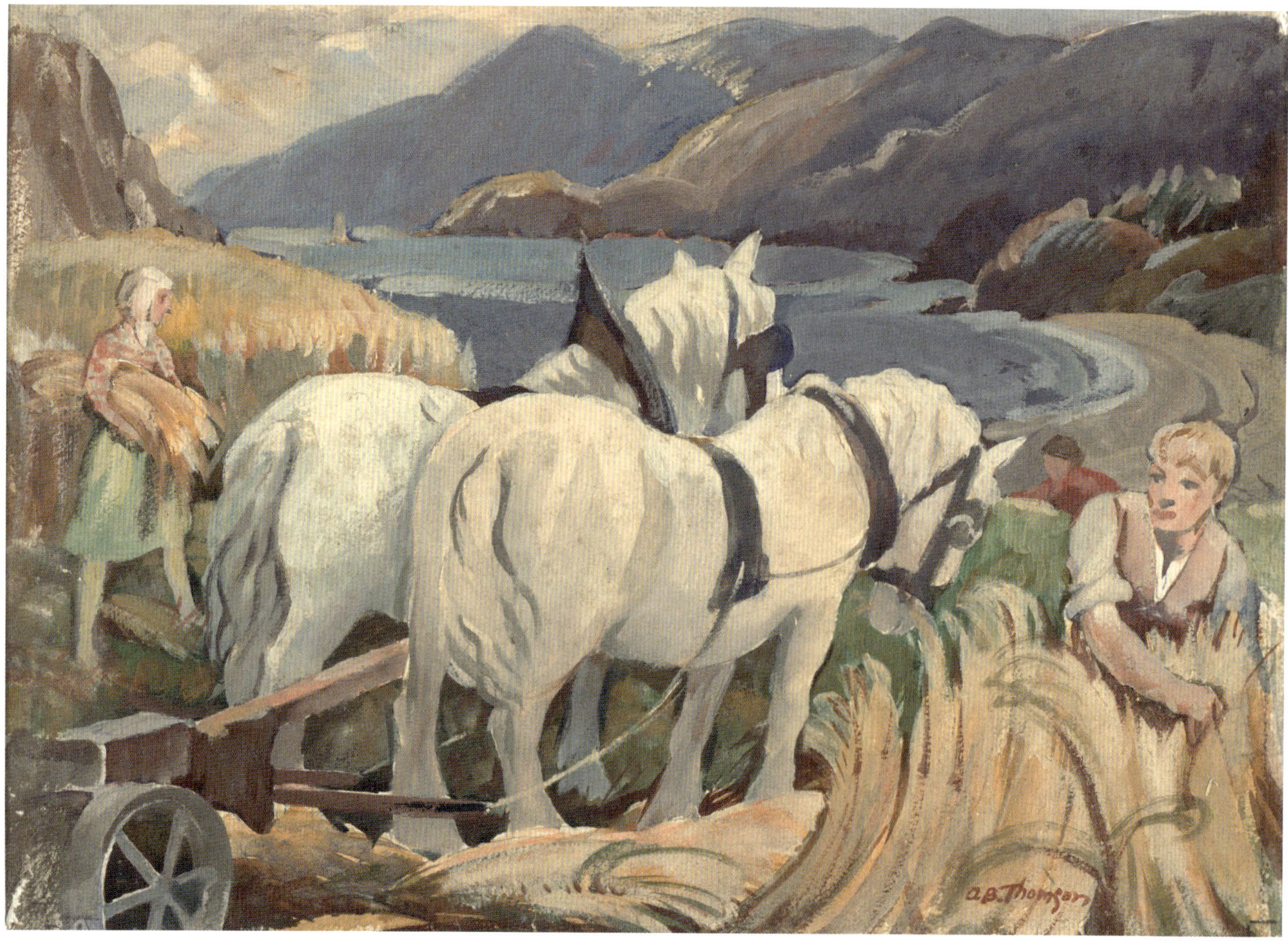

Fig. 30 Adam Bruce Thomson, *Bringing in the Hay*, 1920s. Private Collection. © The artist's estate. (Photograph: Antonia Reeve)

closer to mutual friends like William Gillies and William MacTaggart. Both had studied at Edinburgh College of Art under Thomson, before joining the teaching staff in 1925 and 1933 respectively. Relationships were also strengthened with his long-term associate D.M. Sutherland, and younger colleagues Donald Moodie, Penelope Beaton and John Maxwell. As a group, they sustained and motivated each other, personally and professionally.

Thomson was invigorated by his peers in Edinburgh, but he was also stimulated by the city itself. The historic architecture of the Old Town, the industrial heritage of the suburbs, and the undulating local geography of hills, dells and waterways were sources of endless fascination.

Many of his pre-war drawings and etchings depict Edinburgh views. This interest was renewed following his release from the army, though by the late 1920s he had moved away from printmaking to concentrate on painting.[60]

Working in oils gave Thomson the opportunity to portray the city on a hitherto unrealised scale, imbuing the subject with a more emphatic sense of grandeur and weight. He took up this challenge in the early 1930s, embarking on a series of monumental vistas. *The Old Dean Bridge* (c.1932, Pl. 18) is a significant canvas from the period. It demonstrates the artist's ongoing penchant for combining Cubist forms with an expressive handling of light and shade. The composition is carefully arranged, leading the viewer's gaze up the river and past the bridge to the towering tenements beyond. A palpable tension is present – despite the historic architecture, the deserted scene feels strikingly modern. It was unveiled in 1932 at the annual Royal Scottish Academy exhibition and promptly sold to a private buyer.[61]

Another impressive painting from the series is *North Bridge and Salisbury Crags, Edinburgh, from the North West* (c.1934, Pl. 19). Here again, the artist presents a compelling view of the city, with Arthur's Seat overlooking the dense, shadowy structures of the Old Town. While the lower half is underpinned by the rigid geometry of the built environment, the upper section of hillside terrain seems to expand upwards and outwards into the sunlight. Thomson's contemporaries recognised the importance of this picture when it was exhibited in December 1934. Shortly after going on display, it was purchased by the Society of Scottish Artists and formally presented to the Town Council in order that it might remain permanently accessible to local citizens. The Lord Provost confirmed they would be 'very pleased' to accept the gift.[62]

Over the years, Thomson turned his attention to different parts of Edinburgh, seeking to convey a variety of topographies and environs. Family links to the Colinton area meant the south-west of the city featured often in his work.[63] Residential streets, neighbourhood churches, mature trees and old bridges supplied plentiful subject-matter. Walks through public parks and gardens offered further creative possibilities, and he never seemed to tire of depicting Arthur's Seat. In all weathers and seasons, he delighted in his immediate surroundings.

LANDSCAPES ACROSS SCOTLAND

Thomson's enthusiasm for landscape art was not restricted to his home city. In fact, rural views make up the majority of his *oeuvre* (Fig. 30). Throughout his career he found inspiration in travel, and the Scottish countryside provided a wealth of locations to explore, from the rolling fields of the Lowlands to the rugged peaks of the Highlands.

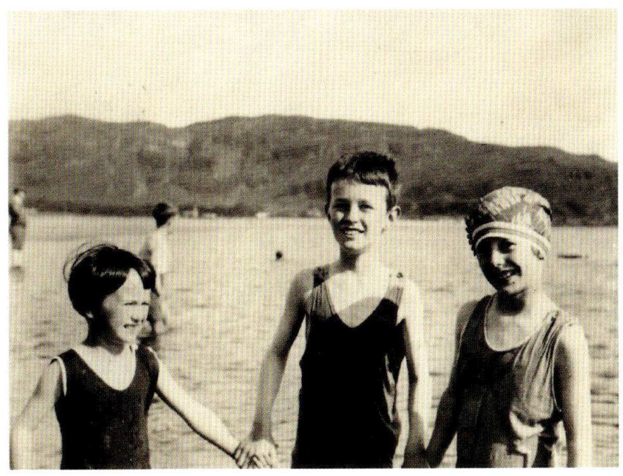

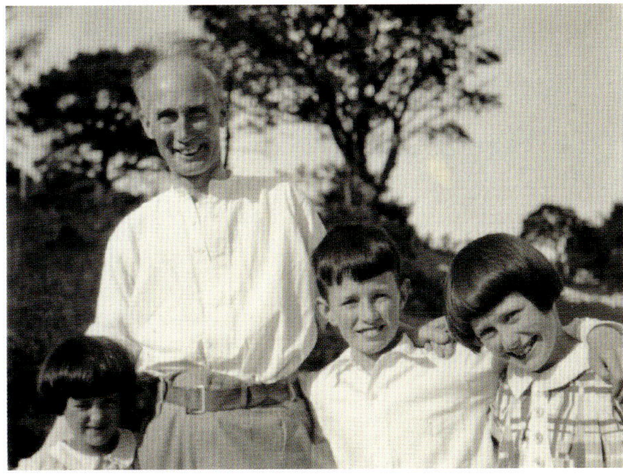

Fig. 31 *(top)* Unknown Photographer, *Mary, Ronald and Margaret at a Beach*, late 1920s. Private Collection.

Fig. 32 *(bottom)* Unknown Photographer, *Adam Bruce Thomson with His Children*, late 1920s. Private Collection.

Prior to the First World War, he made regular excursions to the Dumfries and Galloway region, where he produced meticulous drawings of farm buildings and the ruins of Sweetheart Abbey (Pl. 5). He returned with his wife and children in the 1920s, executing a series of pastel studies around Castle Douglas and the Solway Firth. Family holidays became opportunities for sketching and painting, alongside picnics, walks and other outdoor activities. Photographs suggest these were idyllic times. The children are shown playing on grassy banks and braced for swimming at the beach. Jessie smiles at the camera, while Thomson himself appears happy and relaxed.

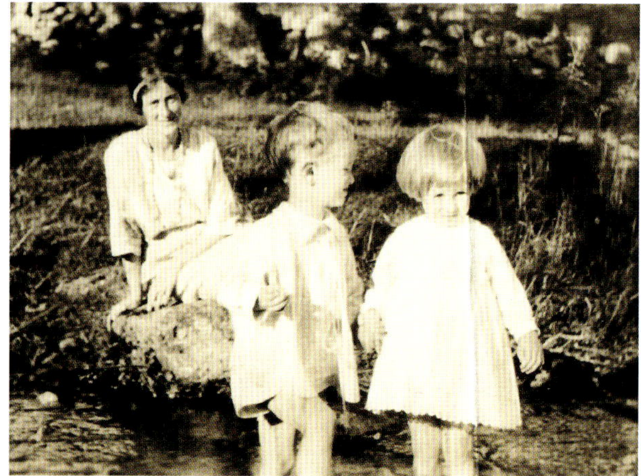

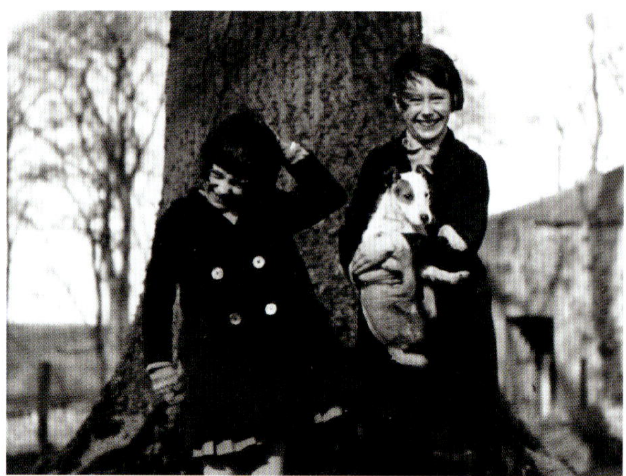

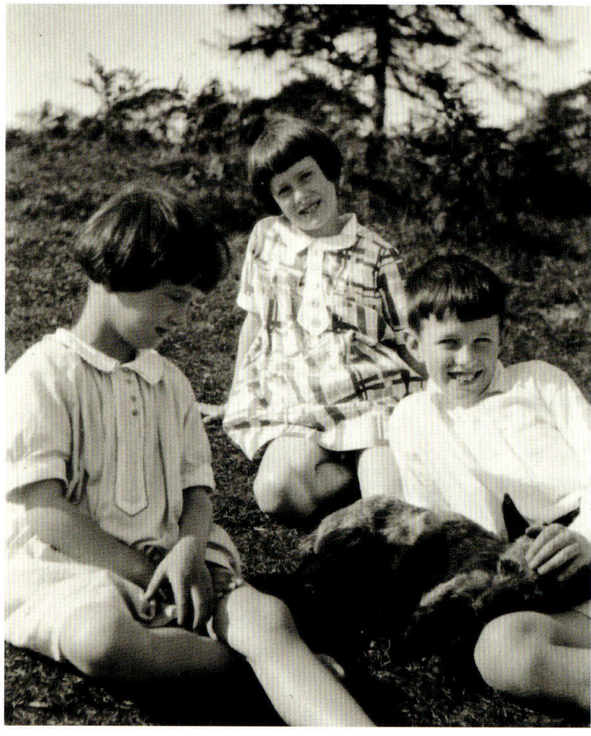

Long summer vacations for staff at Edinburgh College of Art allowed them to make the most of these sojourns, staying away for weeks at a time (Figs. 31–35).

During the early 1930s they joined D.M. Sutherland and his family for holidays in the village of Taynuilt in Argyll. Sutherland had married the artist Dorothy Johnstone in 1924, and their two children, Iain and Anne, were comparable ages to Ronald, Margaret and Mary.[64] The rural setting offered freedom for the youngsters and an array of picturesque subjects to paint. Indeed, Thomson stayed in North Argyll on a number of occasions, with holidays at Benderloch, Port Appin and Ardchattan on the shore of Loch Etive. One of the largest compositions to result from these trips was *The Road to Ben Cruachan* (c.1932, Pl. 20), an imposing mountain scene that is similar in tone to his monumental Edinburgh views of the same period.

Like many artists before him, Thomson was also drawn to the Hebrides. He visited Skye at least as early as 1922. In the autumn of 1923 he displayed *Loch Scavaig and the Cuillins, Skye* at the annual exhibition of the Royal Glasgow Institute. Then in 1925 he showed a further two works, *In Skye* and *Blaven*, at the Royal Scottish Academy. He continued to travel there in later life, painting in Torrin and Kyleakin, where he was particularly interested in the ruined fortress of Caisteal Maol (Pl. 31). Lismore was another Hebridean island that prompted a sizable body of work. Thomson took his family there in 1937 and 1938, spending the summer holidays at Baligrundle Farm. He became quite established within the community, forming a friendship with the local minister, Reverend Calum MacCorquodale (Fig. 38).

Fig. 33 *(top)* Adam Bruce Thomson, *Jessie, Ronald and Margaret by a River*, early to mid-1920s. Private Collection.

Fig. 34 *(middle)* Unknown Photographer, *Mary and Margaret with a Dog*, early 1930s. Private Collection.

Fig. 35 *(bottom)* Unknown Photographer, *Margaret, Mary and Ronald with a Dog*, late 1920s. Private Collection.

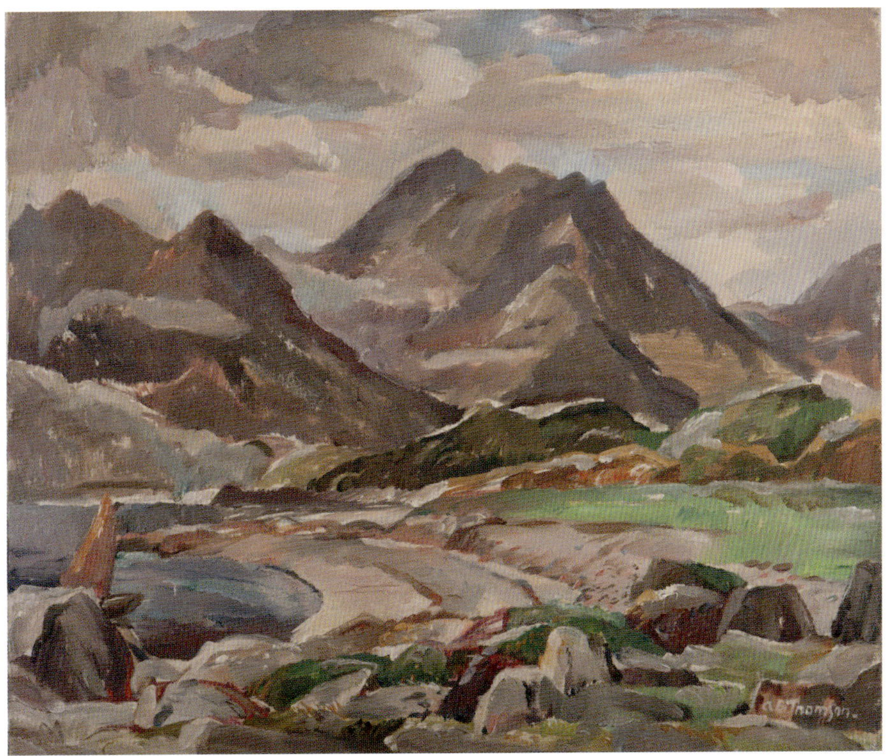

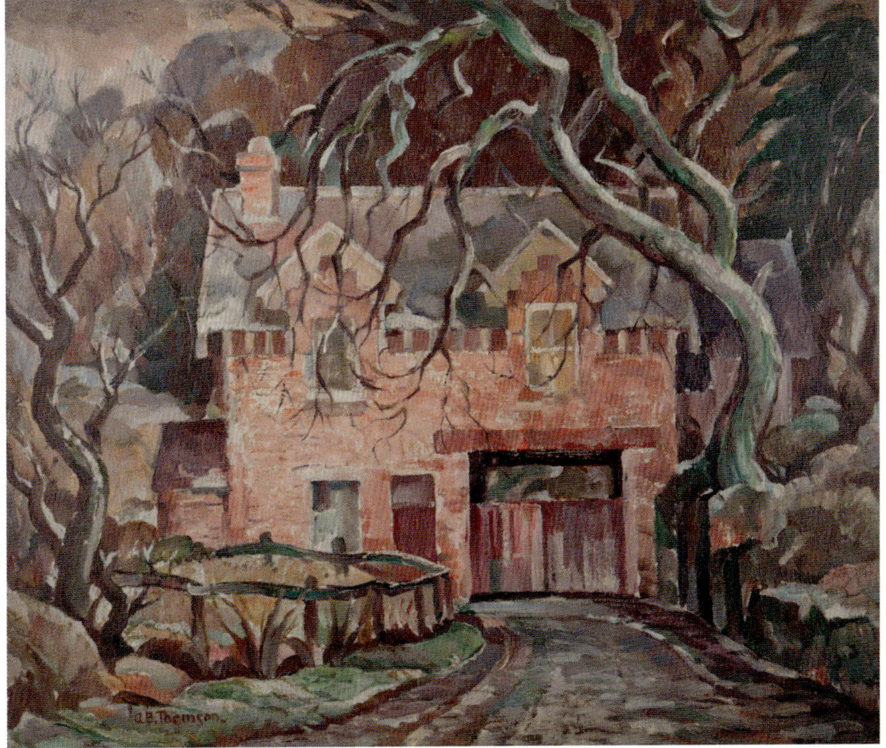

Fig. 36 *(top)* Adam Bruce Thomson, *Argyllshire Landscape, c.*1932.
Private Collection. © The artist's estate. (Photograph: The Scottish Gallery)

Fig. 37 *(bottom)* Adam Bruce Thomson, *Woodland Farm*, 1930s.
Private Collection. © The artist's estate. (Photograph: The Scottish Gallery)

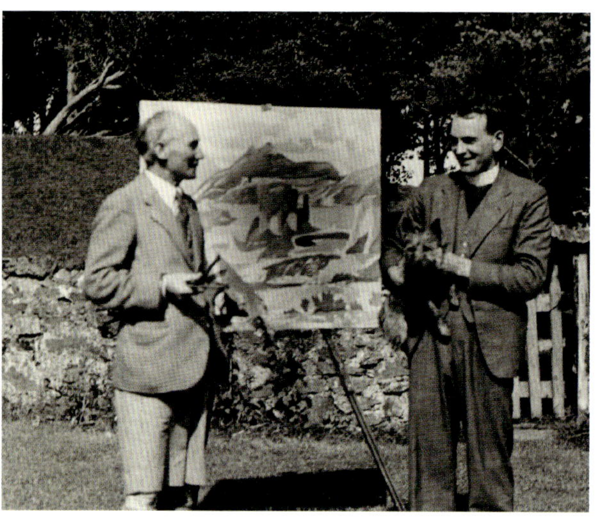

Fig. 38 Unknown Photographer, *Adam Bruce Thomson and Reverend Calum MacCorquodale, Lismore*, c.1937–8. Private Collection.

Decades later, MacCorquodale wrote to the artist reminiscing about his time there. 'It did Lismore good just to have you "in the midst"', he remarked, adding 'They never forgot you.'[65]

In subsequent years Wester Ross emerged as a favourite destination. This scenic part of the north-west Highlands is known for its spectacular mountains, coastal sea lochs and remote settlements. The area was popular with many Edinburgh artists. William Gillies and John Maxwell camped in the district in the mid-1930s, meeting up with D.M. Sutherland and Dorothy Johnstone, who regularly rented a house near Plockton.[66] It is not known when Thomson first visited, though it is likely he was encouraged to do so by friends. By the mid-1940s he was exhibiting artworks based on the landscapes around Shieldaig and Torridon (Pl. 30).[67] He also spent increasing amounts of time in the village of Plockton. Like D.M. Sutherland, he found the local community welcoming and enjoyed walking in the area, discovering new vantage points around Loch Carron. The location, and its changeable weather conditions, inspired countless depictions of the shoreline, cottages and distant mountain views (Fig. 39).

Thomson also worked closer to home. The rich countryside and historic architecture of the Scottish Borders had attracted him since his youth, and these became ever more important subjects in later life.[68] Similarly, the east coast harbours of St Abbs and Eyemouth afforded stimulating vistas within easy reach of Edinburgh (Pl. 29). He also painted in St Monans and Pittenweem in the East Neuk of Fife, fishing villages frequented by friends such as William Gillies and William Wilson.

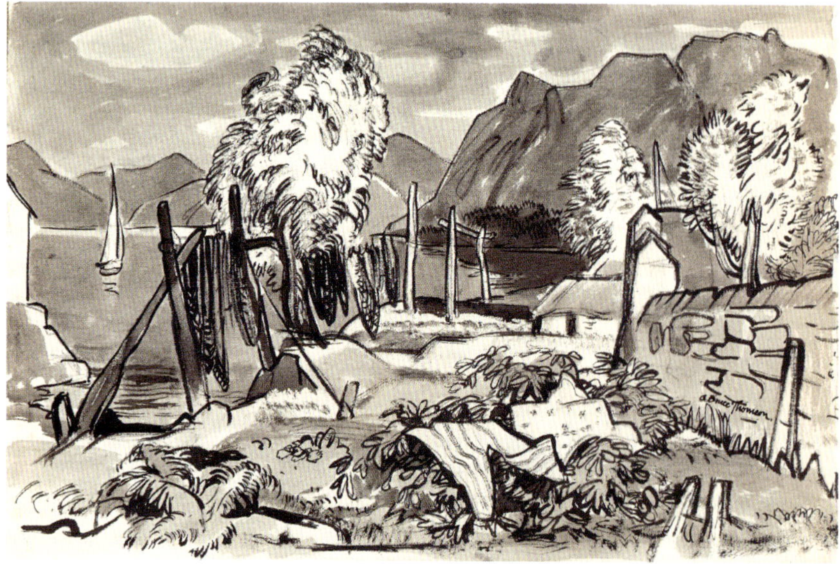

Fig. 39 Adam Bruce Thomson, *Drying the Nets, Plockton*, 1950. Private Collection. © The artist's estate. (Photograph: The Scottish Gallery)

Thomson's expressive landscapes struck a chord with art collectors and critics. From the mid-1920s onwards they constituted the majority of his submissions to public exhibitions and provided most of his sales. In December 1929 he sold an oil painting entitled *On the Ballachulish Line* to Walter Blackie, the successful publisher who had commissioned the Hill House in Helensburgh from the architect Charles Rennie Mackintosh (1868–1928).[69] Attracting the attention of such lucrative clients stood Thomson in good stead. Within ten years his artworks were being referenced regularly in exhibition reviews, and he was being hailed as one of the 'leaders of the modern movement of to-day'.[70]

BUILDING A REPUTATION

The late 1930s were years of steady professional progress. In 1936 Thomson became President of the Society of Scottish Artists. He had been involved with the Society for over twenty years, contributing his first work to the annual exhibition in 1912.[71] As President, he endeavoured to uphold its progressive reputation, using his speech at the opening of the 1936 exhibition as a platform to defend Modernist trends. Offering advice to those who were 'puzzled and confused' by elements of modern art, he recommended:

> if a piece of sculpture or a picture seems unusual, I suggest you do not dismiss it off-hand. Having honestly endeavoured to set aside preconceptions, you may see and understand some of the motives of those who, in all sincerity, are contributing to the works of the present day.[72]

This statement may have been prompted by events of previous years. The 1934 SSA exhibition had sparked an acrimonious debate when the artist David Foggie (1878–1948) took exception to the inclusion of avant-garde works by Paul Klee, a showcase organised by the then President William MacTaggart. Writing in *The Scotsman*, Foggie gave a scathing assessment,

concluding that 'there is not a single work of the twenty-five that has any pictorial significance whatsoever'.[73] The disarming tone of Thomson's speech two years later was perhaps intended to reconcile the two sides of the argument. He was, after all, a colleague of both Foggie and MacTaggart at Edinburgh College of Art. Peace-making aside, his belief in the value of Modernism was genuine; personal notes made on a visit to Paris the following summer describe artworks by Picasso as 'powerful and lucid' and Matisse as 'a lovely colourist'.[74]

In March 1937 Thomson's career received a substantial boost when he was elected as an Associate of the Royal Scottish Academy. This was not the first time he had been nominated. Records reveal that his name was proposed on at least six occasions before he was finally successful.[75] Although the traditionalism of the Academy frustrated some groups, it was still considered a cornerstone of Scotland's artistic establishment, and admission to its ranks was an aspiration for many as a measure of achievement. The painters William MacTaggart and W.O. Hutchison (1889–1970), and the architect Leslie Grahame Thomson (1896–1974), were also elected as Associates on the same day. All four featured in the accompanying press coverage with biographical profiles and photographs.[76]

The prestige associated with membership of the RSA helped Thomson to secure fresh professional opportunities. Not long after his election, he was commissioned to create a 'decorative panel' for the new Head Office of the Edinburgh Savings Bank on Hanover Street. The work was unveiled when the building opened in August 1940. It depicted a view from the roof of the bank's former headquarters on the Mound, looking towards Edinburgh Castle, and was prominently positioned inset above the fireplace in the new boardroom. Contemporary photographs show the panel to be a considerable size (Fig. 40). Measuring almost two metres in width, it was probably his biggest composition to date.[77]

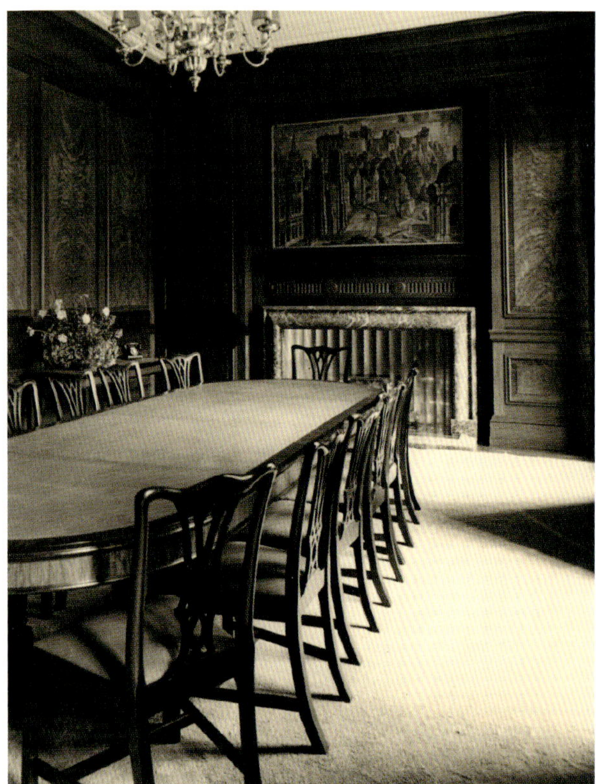

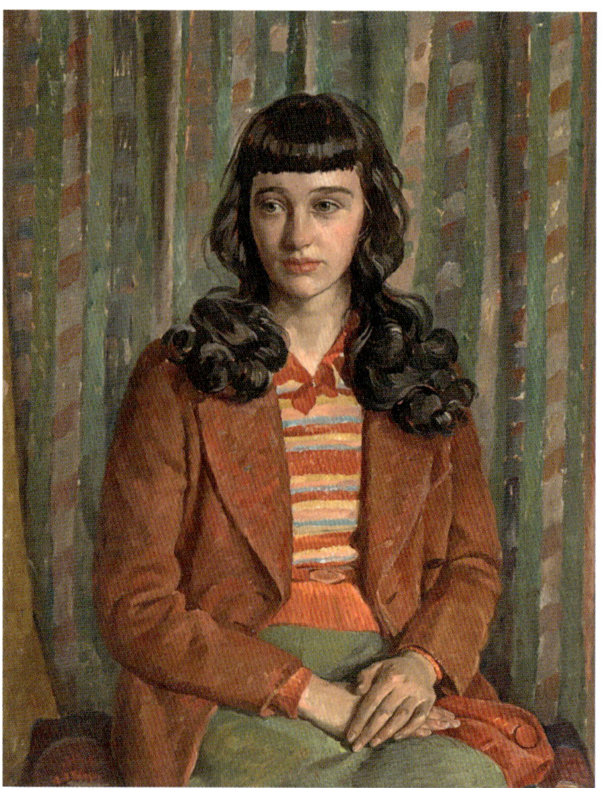

Fig. 40 Unknown Photographer, *Edinburgh Savings Bank Boardroom, Hanover Street (featuring decorative panel by Adam Bruce Thomson)*, August 1940. Private Collection.

Fig. 41 Adam Bruce Thomson, *Mary*, late 1930s. Private Collection. © The artist's estate. (Photograph: Antonia Reeve)

Thomson also received a growing number of portrait commissions. During the early part of the 1930s his work in this genre essentially revolved around family. As infants, his three children were normally captured only in hasty sketches, but as they matured, they were able to pose for longer, becoming subjects for large-scale oil paintings (Fig. 41). These works won critical acclaim. In 1936 a study of his youngest daughter seated in an armchair, *Mary* (1936, Pl. 22), was reproduced in the *Daily Record* to publicise the opening of the SSA annual exhibition. A few months later a portrait of his son, *Ronald* (*c*.1937, Pl. 23), was reviewed positively in *The Scotsman*.[78] Thomson's skill and sensitivity in recording a likeness was widely appreciated, encouraging him to expand his practice. He painted several formal portraits in the 1940s, with sitters including the writer and academic Dr Arthur Melville Clark and the philosopher Professor Norman Kemp Smith. The latter commission was instructed in December 1945 to mark the retirement of Kemp Smith from the Chair of Logic and Metaphysics at the University of Edinburgh.[79] Thomson was asked to execute two portraits, one for the sitter and another to hang in the University (Pl. 28). Kemp Smith must have been impressed; he went on to buy one of the artist's Wester Ross landscapes in November 1946.[80]

WAR RETURNS

Sadly, Thomson's professional achievements at this time were overshadowed by wider events. The outbreak of the Second World War in September 1939 heralded another period of devastating losses, and for those who had experienced the First World War it must have brought back painful memories.

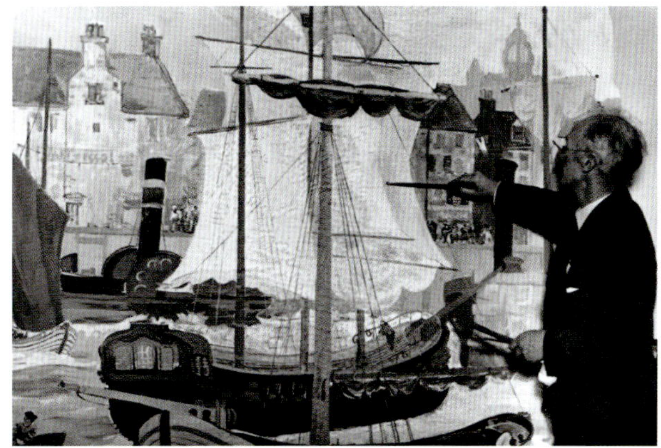

Fig. 42 Unknown Photographer, *Adam Bruce Thomson with Mural at 'The Keel Row', Leith*, 1941. Private Collection.

Once again, Edinburgh College of Art felt the effects of the conflict. Staff and students began to enlist for military service, while air raid shelters were created in the basement and storerooms, and studio windows were blacked out. The College Principal, Hubert Wellington (1879–1967), observed in the 1939–40 Annual Report that it was an unsettling time, noting that: 'the general shock and uncertainties of the opening months made concentration on studies a difficult task'.[81] Thomson carried on teaching those students who remained, trying to maintain favourable learning conditions despite frequent staff changes and classrooms being repurposed.

By this point he was in his mid-fifties and beyond the age of conscription. However, like many older colleagues, he felt compelled to contribute to the war effort. One of the projects the College engaged in was arranging mural decorations for communal feeding centres, known as City Restaurants, which were established in the early years of the war to provide mass cooking and dining facilities for local communities. In Edinburgh, the first City Restaurant opened in Fountainbridge in the spring of 1941, featuring murals designed by Donald Moodie. Thomson was tasked with decorating the second facility, which was called 'The Keel Row' and located within Couper Street School in Leith.[82] He already had some experience of mural painting, having executed a scheme in tempera for Methil Parish Church in Fife in December 1940. For 'The Keel Row', he devised scenes based on Leith's maritime heritage, incorporating images of historic trading ships in a harbour and colourfully dressed Newhaven fishwives (Fig. 42, Fig. 43).

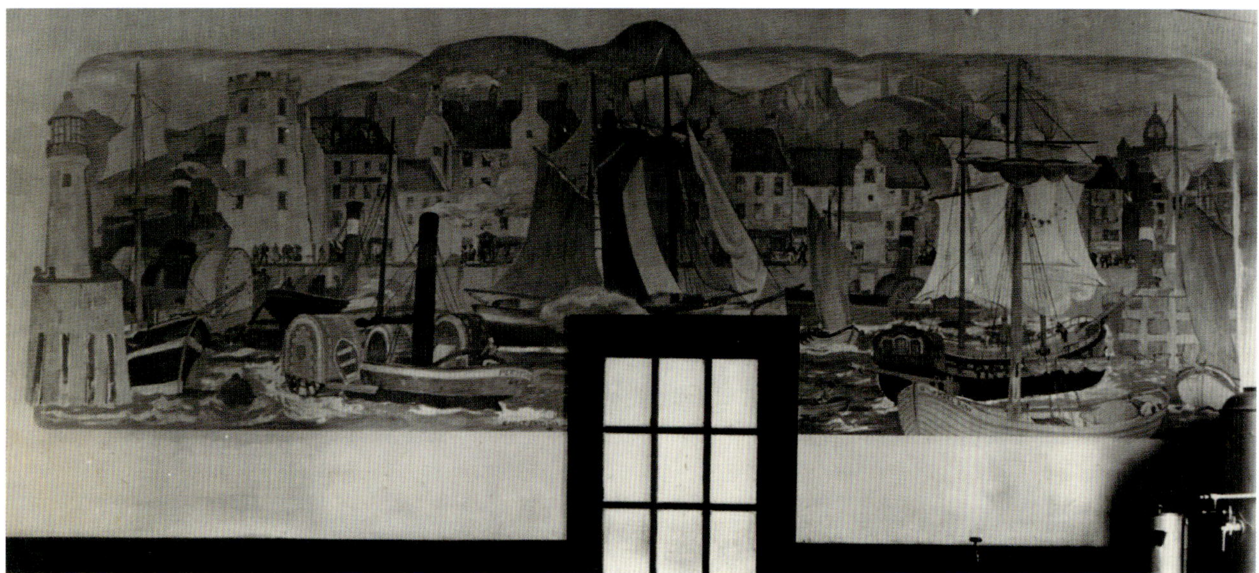

Fig. 43 Unknown Photographer, *Mural by Adam Bruce Thomson at 'The Keel Row', Leith*, June 1942. Private Collection.

The murals were painted in July 1941, with the assistance of two students. According to press reports, they 'attracted much attention' when the building was opened by the Lord Provost.[83]

Such morale-boosting initiatives offered a welcome distraction from the realities of day-to-day life. For Thomson, the strain of the war was compounded by his own personal circumstances. In 1939 his 19-year-old son had been conscripted into the army. Little is known of the details of Ronald's military service, but in early 1940 he suffered a mental breakdown and had to return home. He was admitted to the Crichton Royal Institution, a specialist mental health facility in Dumfries, where he was diagnosed with schizophrenia. Ronald remained as a patient there for the rest of his life. Surviving letters show that he corresponded regularly with his parents and sisters, who often visited and sent presents.[84] The severity of his illness, however, was a profound source of sorrow for the family.

RECOGNITION

After the war, Thomson was elected as a full member of the Royal Scottish Academy. His promotion to the rank of Academician took place in February 1946 and was reported in the Scottish press. Covering the story, *The Bulletin* characterised him as 'a leading exponent of the contemporary point of view'.[85] His ongoing contribution to the country's artistic community was gaining recognition. As T.J. Honeyman, the Director of Kelvingrove Art Gallery in Glasgow, wrote in 1943, he had 'helped to make Edinburgh the centre of the progressive spirit'.[86] Indeed, Thomson's name was increasingly cited in reference to the emerging concept of the 'Edinburgh School'. This grouping was a fluid network of painters rather than a defined set or organised movement. At its heart were prominent figures such as Anne Redpath, William Gillies, William MacTaggart and John Maxwell, later augmented by younger artists including Robin Philipson and Perpetua Pope (1916–2013). They shared the common trait of having studied at Edinburgh College of Art, where many of them continued to teach. Stylistically, they were linked by their expressive treatment of colour and line, as well as their preference for landscape and still-life subjects.[87]

Throughout the 1940s the commercial Scottish Gallery, operated by the dealership Aitken Dott & Son, invited artists associated with the Edinburgh School to stage solo exhibitions in their premises at 26 Castle Street. Thomson's turn came a few months after his election as an Academician. Between 21 October and 2 November 1946, he presented 66 watercolours at the Scottish Gallery in his first ever solo show. Most of the artworks were landscapes, depicting views of Wester Ross, Berwickshire, Perthshire and other locations. The exhibition was well received. One critic described it as an 'extraordinarily lively show', adding 'there is a rare swing about some of these sketches, and a sense of wind and sun'.[88] Apparently, almost everything sold.[89]

The fact that this exhibition was comprised entirely of watercolours was no accident. Artists of the Edinburgh School tended to place as much emphasis on works on paper as they did on oil paintings, subverting the traditional viewpoint that watercolours were a less serious, or even amateur, form of expression. Thomson subscribed to this shift in attitude. During the post-war period he devoted significant amounts of time to watercolours, experimenting with different techniques and combining the medium with ink drawing. His painting style became looser and more spontaneous, while still retaining the awareness of compositional structure he had developed through his practice in oils. Working outdoors, in direct contact with nature and the elements, he seemed to find a new spirit of freedom. In 1947 he joined the Royal Scottish Society of Painters in Watercolour (RSW), an organisation dedicated to promoting the medium. He contributed regularly to their exhibitions and served for many years as a committed member, ultimately being elected as President.[90]

MOVING ON

Towards the end of the 1940s, Thomson started to consider his retirement from teaching at Edinburgh College of Art. By this stage, William Gillies had replaced David Alison as Head of the School of Drawing and Painting, and Robin Philipson had been appointed to the staff. The curriculum remained largely unchanged, with a continuing stress on the importance of traditional draughtsmanship and painting techniques. The prevailing philosophy was that students should not be allowed to experiment until they had mastered the basics. Some chaffed at the strictures of this academic approach, judging their tutors to be old-fashioned and out-of-touch. Latterly, Thomson was among those to attract such complaints; his classes in Composition were deemed particularly dry by some students.[91] Yet, over the years, he consistently equipped each cohort with the skills to practise as professional artists. Wilhelmina Barns-Graham (1912–2004), William Gear (1915–1997), Alan Davie (1920–2014), John Houston (1930–2008) and Elizabeth Blackadder (1931–2021) are just a few examples of the many successful painters who trained under him. Indeed, while his standards were exacting, he was always supportive. Throughout the College he was affectionately known as 'Adam B.'[92]

Thomson's decision to retire in 1950 was not entirely voluntary. College rules dictated that male members of staff could not work beyond the age of 65, while women had to retire at 60. Some colleagues, such as Penelope Beaton, protested against these regulations, applying to have their contracts extended.[93] Thomson enjoyed teaching and may have stayed longer had the age limit not existed. He did not contest the situation, however, and was apparently content to leave at the end of the academic year.

In the event, his departure was only temporary. In May 1951 he joined the College's Board of Management, representing the Royal Scottish Academy alongside Anne Redpath and William Wilson. In this role he was involved in

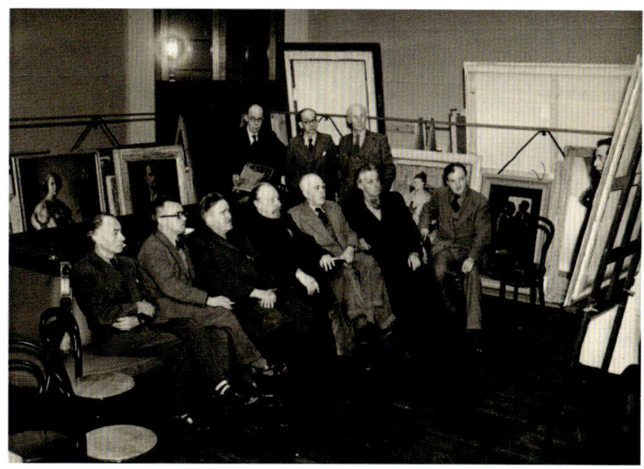

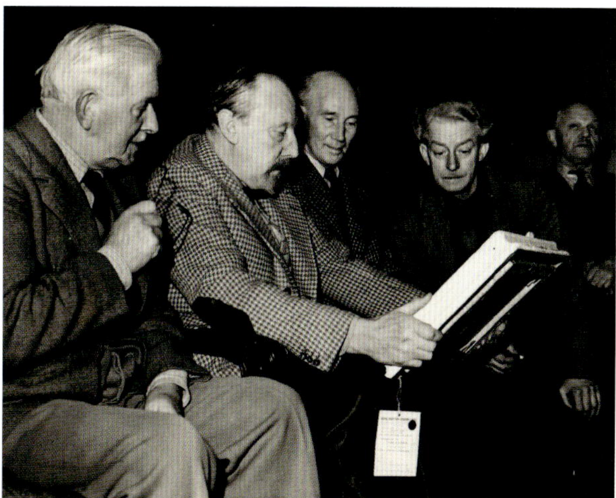

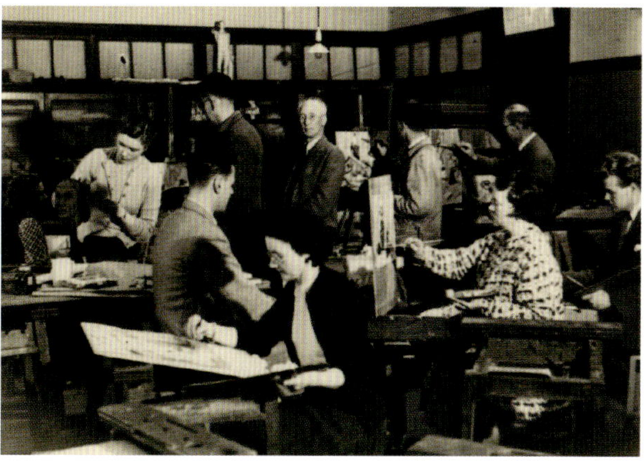

Fig. 44 *(top)* Unknown Photographer, *Royal Scottish Academy Annual Exhibition Selection Committee, Edinburgh* (Adam Bruce Thomson in back row, far right), early 1950s. Private Collection.

Fig. 45 *(middle)* Unknown Photographer, *Royal Scottish Academy Annual Exhibition Selection Committee, Edinburgh* (left to right: D.M. Sutherland, W.O. Hutchison, Adam Bruce Thomson, William Gillies, R. Moncrieff), 1950s. Private Collection.

Fig. 46 *(bottom)* George F. Smith, *Adam Bruce Thomson Teaching at Stornoway Art Club*, 1951. Private Collection.

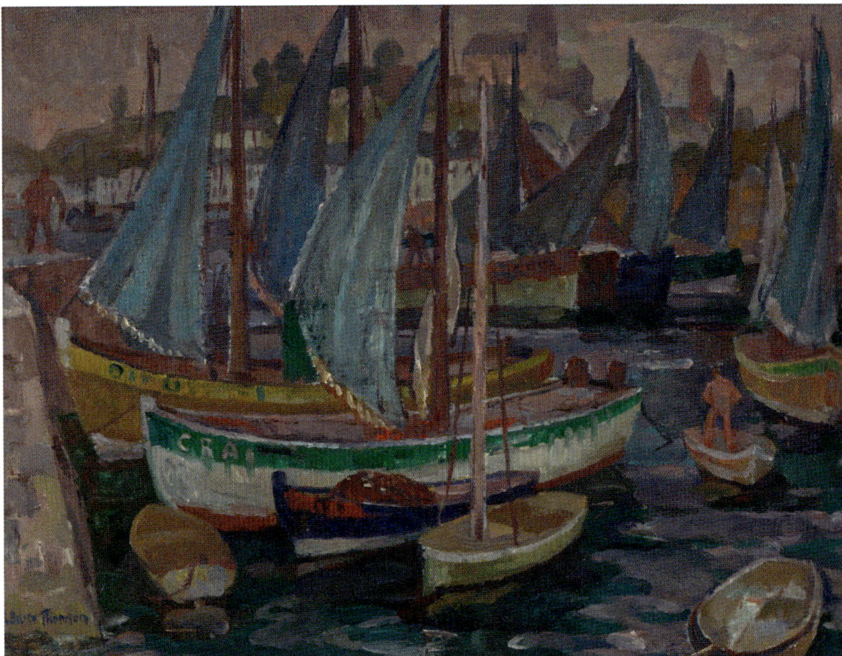

a range of matters, from advising on building alterations to assessing scholarship applications.[94] He subsequently became part of the Adjudication Committee for the Award of Diplomas in Drawing and Painting, examining students' final-year work. After three years he stood down, but was persuaded to return in 1960 when William Gillies took over as Principal of the College. Thomson carried on as an Adjudicator until Gillies himself retired in 1966.

He showed an equal degree of commitment to artist-led societies. Between 1949 and 1956 he served as Treasurer of the RSA. In this capacity one of his many contributions was to lay the foundations for the establishment of the John Kinross Memorial Trust.[95] Thomson entered into lengthy negotiations with John Blythe Kinross over the formation of the Trust, which was envisaged to commemorate the financier's father, the architect John Kinross (1855–1931). The complexities of the project were extensive. When Thomson eventually stood down as Treasurer, the Secretary of the RSA, William MacTaggart, wrote to thank him for his dedication, commenting that the work 'went far beyond the normal duties' of his office, and that its success owed much to his 'skill and tact'.[96]

Thomson replied that it had been his privilege to advance an initiative that would benefit future artists.

Throughout this period, he acted as a selector for the annual exhibitions of the RSA (Fig. 44, Fig. 45). He also maintained his support of the Royal Scottish Society of Painters in Watercolour, taking on the role of President in 1956. Two years later he was appointed as Honorary President of the Edinburgh Sketching Club, a local society he had encouraged for some time. He even engaged in further teaching, instructing classes in still-life painting at the Stornoway Art Club in 1951, a project funded by the Carnegie Trust (Fig. 46). He regarded his ongoing involvement in the artistic community as a matter of personal duty.[97]

Despite these commitments, Thomson still found time for his own creative practice. After his retirement from the College, he was able to travel more frequently, seeking out inspiration in different locations. In about 1950 he undertook a rare family holiday abroad, visiting the coastal resort of Tréboul in Brittany (Fig. 47). Later, in the early 1960s, he and his wife Jessie explored the Cotswolds while staying in the market town of Chipping Campden.[98] Such trips resulted in a number of sketches and paintings, but it was Scottish destinations that continued to provide the most potent wellspring of ideas. His introduction to Stornoway sparked several return visits to the Isle of Lewis, where he focused on the bustling activity of Stornoway harbour (Pl. 32) and the atmospheric setting of the Calanais Standing Stones. His long-term interest in history and archaeology also led him to concentrate on the ruined abbeys of the Scottish Borders, working in Melrose, Dryburgh and Kelso. Quite often he combined these architectural subjects with depictions of surrounding woodland, as in *Park and Ruined Abbey* (*c*.1961, Pl. 33), which he selected as his submission to the RSA Diploma Collection.[99]

Thomson exhibited his paintings widely, and sold to a range of buyers. By the early 1960s he was making fairly regular sales to public collections as well as private individuals. Dundee Art Gallery, Kelvingrove Art Gallery and the City of Edinburgh were among the local government authorities to acquire his compositions. While his principal audience remained the Scottish art market, his reputation was beginning to reach further afield. Sales records show that in 1960 he sold a picture of Tarbert in Argyll to a buyer from Canada.[100]

ENDURING FRIENDSHIPS

In November 1962 Thomson learned that he had been recommended to receive an OBE in the New Year Honours List. News of the award appeared in the press on 2 January 1963, and he was soon inundated with congratulatory letters from friends, colleagues and former students. One of the first to write was D.M. Sutherland, followed shortly by William MacTaggart, William Gillies and William Wilson. Although Thomson had known about the forthcoming announcement for some weeks, he does not appear to have told friends in advance – almost everyone expressed surprise when they wrote to him. Sutherland gave an especially detailed account of his discovery in the morning newspaper. He remarked that he was 'totally unprepared' to find his friend's photograph there,

adding that 'immediately the Honours List took on a very special importance'.[101] Sutherland may have been caught off-guard by the news, but he was probably unsurprised by Thomson's reticence to flaunt his achievement. He was well aware of his friend's modesty.

Thomson and Sutherland had known each other since their student days on the Mound. The pair kept in contact when Sutherland left Edinburgh in 1933 to become Principal of Gray's School of Art in Aberdeen, and they corresponded frequently after retirement. During the 1960s and early 1970s they wrote to each other at least once a week.[102] Discussions covered a range of topics, from developments at the Royal Scottish Academy to recent programmes on television. Their individual progress in painting was a regular theme. When Thomson visited Iona in the late 1960s, he recounted the inspirational experience to Sutherland, describing it as a kind of 'magic'. He also confided in him when he was struggling with his art, admitting that he was prone to 'worrying and almost going off my sleep if work wasn't going as I wanted'.[103] They shared advice on both professional and personal matters. Sutherland's heartfelt offers of support regarding Thomson's efforts to cope with the mental illness of his son are particularly moving.

William Wilson was another lifelong companion. Thomson had acted as a mentor to Wilson in the early stages of his career, and was proud to witness his growing success. By the 1950s his former student had become the pre-eminent stained-glass artist in Scotland, as well as an acclaimed printmaker and watercolourist. Over the decades the pair spent much time together, whether socialising or contributing to various committees. They often exchanged artworks as gifts. In later life, Wilson developed diabetes and started to lose his sight. Thomson visited often as his friend's health deteriorated. Concerned for his well-being amidst escalating money problems, he lobbied the RSA to ensure that Wilson received financial aid in 1971.[104]

Thomson's long-term involvement with artist-led societies meant that he was always well connected. He diligently attended meetings, receptions and exhibition openings throughout his retirement years. Upon reaching his eighties, however, he found that a full diary had diminishing appeal. As he confessed to D.M. Sutherland, 'I still enjoy a sharp walk for half an hour in the dark but too many engagements are not for me.'[105]

FINAL YEARS

In 1965 Thomson and his wife moved to 65 Cluny Gardens, a semi-detached villa near Blackford Hill (Fig. 48). This area of south Edinburgh became a prominent subject in his work, with depictions of Blackford Pond and panoramic views towards Arthur's Seat (Fig. 49, Pl. 40). Thomson had always been a keen walker, and he relished roaming the local upland routes with his sketchbook. On one occasion he fell and broke his knee while descending Blackford Hill. Though his recovery from surgery was slow, he remained determined to continue exploring and painting scenic locations.

Within a year of his accident, he was back in the village of Plockton in Wester Ross (Fig. 50). This trip proved highly productive, inspiring multiple drawings and paintings, including his large-scale canvas *Palm, Pampas Grass and Duncraig* (*c.*1967, Pl. 37). This joyful image portrays a garden in Plockton overlooking Loch Carron. A few years later, Thomson told D.M. Sutherland about its conception:

> The general locality was just opposite from Mrs Moore's […], simply across the road to her little patch of garden. Of an evening when twilight was on the way I used to moon up and down the village gazing across Loch Carron to the opposite hill now becoming quiet and simple […] That picture was the result of these prowlings.[106]

Palm, Pampas Grass and Duncraig was unveiled at the Royal Scottish Academy in 1967, whereupon it was acquired for the City of Edinburgh's art collection. Other recent Plockton landscapes featured that year in a solo exhibition at the Scottish Arts Club. Staged within the Club's Edinburgh premises on Rutland Square, this display opened in late January 1967 and ran until the middle of March. Its full content has not yet been established, but records indicate that Thomson's biggest sale came from the purchase of his oil painting *The Path to Duncraig*, which was bought by the Standard Life Assurance Company for £80.[107]

A few months later, he mounted another solo show at the Douglas & Foulis Gallery on Castle Street. This exhibition, held between 20 May and 3 June 1967, presented over forty artworks. There were oils, watercolours and a selection of drawings spanning landscape, portrait and still-life themes. At least 21 of them sold.[108] The display received many positive reviews, with critics commending the freshness of Thomson's watercolours and the clarity of his drawing style. Several highlighted his

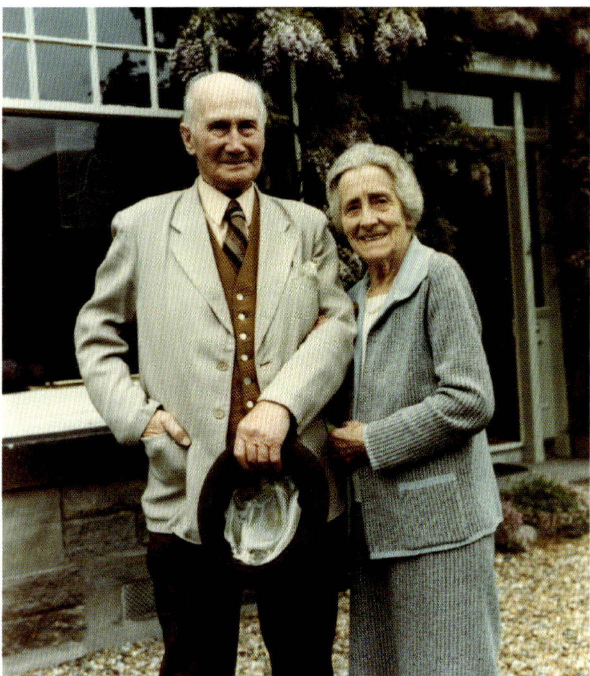

Fig. 48 J. Kinghorn, *Adam Bruce Thomson and Jessie Thomson at 65 Cluny Gardens, Edinburgh*, *c.*1970s. Private Collection.

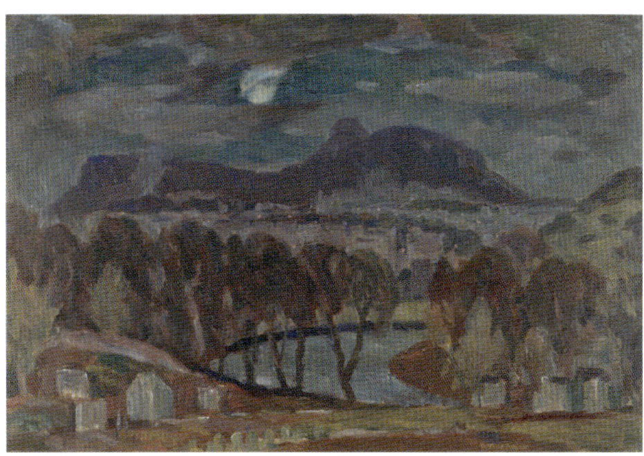

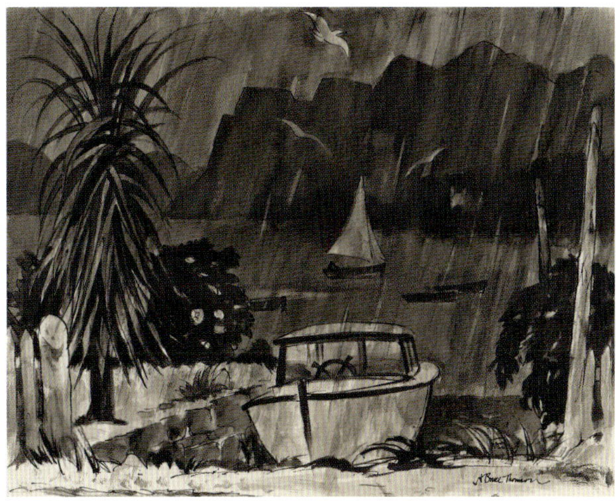

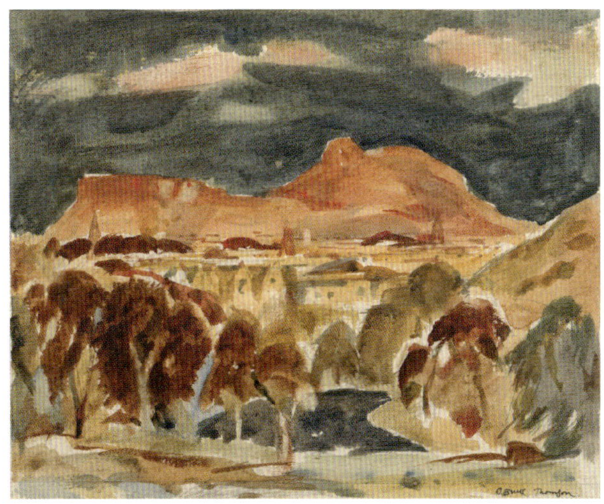

Fig. 49 *(top)* Adam Bruce Thomson, *Arthur's Seat at Night*, 1960s. Private Collection. © The artist's estate. (Photograph: Antonia Reeve)

Fig. 50 *(middle)* Adam Bruce Thomson, *Heavy Weather, Plockton*, *c.*1967. Private Collection. © The artist's estate. (Photograph: The Scottish Gallery)

Fig. 51 *(bottom)* Adam Bruce Thomson, *Arthur's Seat*, early 1970s. City Art Centre, City of Edinburgh Museums and Galleries. © The artist's estate. (Photograph: Antonia Reeve)

wider contribution. As Felix McCullough pointed out in the *Edinburgh Evening News*, Thomson 'has been for so long and so influentially part of Scottish artistic life that it seems scarcely credible that this is only his second solo show'.[109] Afterwards, the veteran artist appraised the experience in typically understated terms. 'I suppose my show might be looked on as successful', he remarked to D.M. Sutherland, quipping: 'I don't think an awful lot about newspaper criticism but it is extraordinary how people seem to go by it.'[110] In spite of this self-deprecation, he must have been inwardly pleased; cuttings of press reviews were kept by his family for posterity.

In December 1970, at the age of 85, Thomson voluntarily retired from the RSA. In a letter to the President, he wrote that his decision had not been prompted by feeling unable to carry out his duties any longer, but rather the hope that his departure would create a vacancy for someone else. As he explained, 'I'm happy to think that by taking this step I am making way for an associate to be elected to full rank and that I am acting in the interests of the Academy.'[111] It was a characteristically selfless act devised to introduce new blood into the organisation. Thomson could not be persuaded to reconsider. His resignation was formally accepted in January 1971 and he became an Honorary Retired Member, a status which still allowed him to participate in RSA exhibitions. He now focused his energies on making and displaying new work.

Over the next six years, he continued to paint the landscapes of Wester Ross, the Scottish Borders and his home city of Edinburgh. Views of Arthur's Seat became a particular preoccupation (Fig. 51).

Thomson was fascinated by the transient effects of changing light and colour on the hill and its urban surroundings, perceiving limitless possibilities in different atmospheric conditions. Studying the outlook by day and night, he recorded his observations in oils and watercolours, gradually reinforcing his understanding of the subject.

In the spring of 1976 he showed two works from this series as part of his submission to the RSA annual exhibition. Both received special attention. The watercolour *Allotments and Arthur's Seat* was purchased for the RSA collection, while the oil painting *Rising Moon: Arthur's Seat* (c.1976) won the inaugural William J. Macaulay Award. This new prize, commemorating the late proprietor of Aitken Dott & Son, was reserved for the 'most distinguished work' in the exhibition. Robin Philipson, then President of the RSA, later told Thomson that his painting had been judged the 'unanimous favourite'.[112] Art critics were equally impressed. Writing for *The Scotsman*, Edward Gage described the brooding landscape as 'really splendid', comparing it to Paul Cézanne's iconic studies of Mont Sainte-Victoire.[113] *Rising Moon: Arthur's Seat* was ultimately sold to a private buyer, though it was shown in public one last time in August 1976, when it featured in a special display marking the 150th anniversary of the RSA.

LEGACY

Adam Bruce Thomson carried on painting and exhibiting into his final months. He died on 4 December 1976 after a short illness, at the age of 91. The previous year, his 90th birthday had been celebrated with a formal dinner at the Royal Scottish Academy organised by Edinburgh College of Art. There were speeches in his honour and a presentation of gifts.[114] This event may have been a bittersweet affair. Although Thomson was surrounded by well-wishers, and accompanied by his wife and eldest daughter, there were notable absences. His old friends William Wilson, William Gillies and D.M. Sutherland had all passed away in the early 1970s. Thomson was one of the last

survivors. At least he would have been left in little doubt regarding the affection and esteem in which he was held by Edinburgh's artistic community. In the words of Dr Arthur Melville Clark, who delivered a toast that night, he was 'our beloved and patriarchal Adam'.[115]

In 1977 both the Royal Scottish Academy and the Royal Scottish Society of Painters in Watercolour mounted small displays as posthumous tributes to Thomson. Artworks were lent by public collections, friends and the artist's family, representing some of the highlights of his career. In later years, his daughters, Margaret and Mary, did much to promote their father's professional reputation. They began the process of cataloguing his artworks, preserved an archive of written material, and worked with the Scottish Gallery to arrange a major exhibition for his centenary in 1985.[116] A selection of drawings, paintings and prints were also donated to public institutions, including the National Library of Scotland and the National Galleries of Scotland.[117]

As an artist, Thomson was highly motivated and prolific. Over the course of his life, he produced and sold many hundreds of artworks, only a small proportion of which have so far been traced by researchers. Some have been lost to posterity. Others are held in private collections, enjoyed by owners across the country and further afield, some of whom are perhaps unaware of their attributions.

This well-dispersed *oeuvre* forms a substantial part of Thomson's legacy, but it is not the sole component. He also left a series of less tangible contributions. Throughout his forty-year teaching career at Edinburgh College of Art, he trained and supported successive cohorts of students, from William Gillies to Elizabeth Blackadder, from Anne Redpath to James Cumming (1922–1991). Several of these students went on to become influential teachers themselves. His service to the College extended beyond his official retirement, a dedication matched by his long-term commitment to artist-led organisations and exhibiting societies. He was always willing to offer his time and expertise, no matter the scale of the cause. This sense of duty further defined his relationships; as a mentor he was ever encouraging, as a companion he was unfailingly loyal.[118] While his impact on the lives and careers of others cannot be measured, it is still clearly significant.

Today, the Adam Bruce Thomson Award is presented annually to outstanding graduates of Scottish art colleges as part of the RSA 'New Contemporaries' exhibition programme. This prize was endowed by Thomson's friend Arthur Melville Clark in 1979, as a means of enabling emerging artists to go on benefiting from his influence. It is an abiding testament to the widespread regard he inspired.[119]

Thomson was an artist of versatility and intellect, whose boundless energy was invariably guided by his integrity. He cherished his family and valued his friends, and would not contemplate putting his career before them. In his lifetime, his reluctance to pursue his own personal advancement often led to him being underestimated and overlooked in favour of more ambitious peers. Even now, he is seldom granted the art historical limelight. Yet this situation is unlikely to have troubled him; recognition and accolades were always honours he was happy to share. Thomson's legacy remains quiet, though it is nonetheless enduring – a heartbeat that pulses through twentieth-century Scottish art, and continues to be felt to this day.

ENDNOTES

1. *Edinburgh College of Art Annual Report by the Board of Management to the Governors for the Session 1949–1950*, p.6. Edinburgh College of Art Archive, Centre for Research Collections, the University of Edinburgh.

2. Edinburgh College of Art Retirement Certificate presented to Adam Bruce Thomson, June 1950, private collection.

3. To date, the most comprehensive piece of art historical writing on Thomson is the catalogue produced by the Scottish Gallery to accompany the exhibition 'Adam Bruce Thomson (1885–1976): Painting the Century', 6–30 November 2013.

4. Guy Peploe, *Adam Bruce Thomson (1885–1976): Painting the Century*, the Scottish Gallery, Edinburgh, 6–30 November 2013, p.3 (exhibition catalogue).

5. See Scottish Census records for 1881, 1891, 1901 and 1911, National Records of Scotland. See also *Post-Office Edinburgh & Leith Directory*, editions 1901–2 through to 1909–10.

6. Thomson's paternal grandfather, Alexander Thomson, was also a cabinetmaker by trade.

7. Also sometimes referred to as the Edinburgh School of Art. For background on the establishment and history of this institution see: David Irwin and Francina Irwin, *Scottish Painters at Home and Abroad 1700–1900*, Faber & Faber, London, 1975, pp.90–97.

8. Surviving certificates awarded by Heriot-Watt College show that Thomson attended evening classes there between at least 1899 and 1903. He obtained distinction grades in Freehand Drawing of Ornament, Perspective and Elementary Design. Heriot-Watt College Class Certificates of Merit, 1899–1903, private collection.

9. Thomson's friend Esme Gordon claimed that his interest in painting supplanted architecture after a 'short period' at the Trustees' School of Art. See: Esme Gordon, 'Adam Bruce Thomson, R.S.A. Obituary', *One Hundredth and Forty-Ninth Annual Report of the Council of the Royal Scottish Academy of Painting, Sculpture and Architecture*, 1976, p.40.

10. Board of Education South Kensington Certificates, 1905–7, private collection.

11. In the photograph, Thomson is positioned in the middle row, second figure from the left with easels behind him. Walter B. Hislop is beside Thomson, directly in front of the nude model. Eric Robertson is seated in the front row, third from the left. A.R. Sturrock appears further along the middle row, second from the right. D.M. Sutherland stands in the back row, furthest to the right. Life Class Photograph, Trustees' School of Art, possibly June 1908, private collection.

12. Robertson was a promising student whose talents were sometimes eclipsed by his tumultuous personal life, see: John Kemplay, *The Two Companions: The Story of Two Scottish Artists Eric Robertson and Cecile Walton*, Ronald Crowhurst, Edinburgh, 1991. Joyce Cary became a writer after training at the Trustees' School of Art, publishing his satirical novel *The Horse's Mouth* in 1944. The book still prompts speculation regarding the identities of the real-life artists who inspired his characters.

13. Barbara Fisher, *Transcript of Interview with Adam Bruce Thomson* (interview conducted at 65 Cluny Gardens, Edinburgh), 25 August 1968, private collection.

14. Letter from Adam Bruce Thomson to D.M. Sutherland, 29 November 1968, private collection.

15. 'Edinburgh Town Council: A New Art School', *The Scotsman*, 12 April 1906, p.8.

16. For more on the establishment of Edinburgh College of Art see: Scott J. Lawrie, *The Edinburgh College of Art (1904–1969): A Study in Institutional History*, Master of Philosophy Thesis, Edinburgh College of Art (Heriot-Watt University), 1996, pp.1–16.

17. Gordon, 'Adam Bruce Thomson, R.S.A. Obituary', p.40. The grievances outlined in the petition were reported in the local press, see: 'Inadequate Accommodation at the Royal Institution School of Art', *The Scotsman*, 7 April 1906, p.8.

18. *Prospectus of the Edinburgh College of Art, Session 1908–1909*, ECA 3/1/1/1. Edinburgh College of Art Archive, Centre for Research Collections, the University of Edinburgh.

19. The construction of Edinburgh College of Art was completed in stages over several years. The entire building was not fully finished until October 1912. See: Duncan Macmillan, *Unpublished Manuscript on the History of Edinburgh College of Art*

1907–1960, c.2007, p.15.

20. Minutes of Meeting of the General Purposes Committee of the Board of Management of the Edinburgh College of Art, 25 September 1908, *Minutes Book of Meetings of Governors, Edinburgh College of Art*, Book 1, March 1908–June 1909, p.86. Edinburgh College of Art Archive, Centre for Research Collections, the University of Edinburgh.

21. Letter of Reference from John Marshall LLD, Rector of Royal High School Edinburgh, 28 May 1908, private collection.

22. Thomson shared the prize with his classmate Albert C. Dodds. See: *Edinburgh College of Art Annual Report by the Board of Management to the Governors for the Session 1908–1909*, p.14. Edinburgh College of Art Archive, Centre for Research Collections, the University of Edinburgh.

23. 'Educational', *The Scotsman*, 21 January 1909, p.11.

24. Thomson's journey can be traced through various surviving documents. See: Adam Bruce Thomson, *Architectural Tour (July 3rd 1909) and Etching Notes and Lithographic Reminders (1915)*, Handwritten Notebook, 1909–15, private collection. See also: Adam Bruce Thomson, *Travelling Scholarships Diary*, September 1909–May 1910, private collection.

25. For at least part of this trip Thomson was accompanied by the architectural artist Hanslip Fletcher and fellow Edinburgh College of Art architectural graduate John B. Lawson, the latter of whom had also received a Travelling Scholarship.

26. *Edinburgh College of Art Student Records Book I*, c.1908–20, ECA 3/2/1/1. Edinburgh College of Art Archive, Centre for Research Collections, the University of Edinburgh. The two other students to receive their Drawing and Painting Diplomas were Walter B. Hislop and Wilma Law Weir, see: *Edinburgh College of Art Annual Report by the Board of Management to the Governors for the Session 1908–1909*, pp.12–13.

27. The details of Thomson's journey are recorded in: Thomson, *Travelling Scholarships Diary*. See also: Adam Bruce Thomson, Handwritten Notebook, 1910–68, private collection.

28. Entry for 11 February 1910. Thomson, *Travelling Scholarships Diary*.

29. Letter from Adam Bruce Thomson to Barbara Fisher, 25 March 1971, private collection. For more on Thomson's time in Paris with Eric Robertson and John Duncan see: Kemplay, *The Two Companions*, pp.13–14.

30. Entries for 13–16 April 1910. Thomson, *Travelling Scholarships Diary*.

31. Entry for 30 April 1910. Ibid. The Spanish leg of Thomson's Travelling Scholarship is further described in: Adam Bruce Thomson, *Travelling Scholarships Diary*, May–June 1910, private collection.

32. The most significant known example is the oil painting *Bridge of St Martin, Toledo*, which Thomson exhibited at the 1911 RSA annual exhibition.

33. Notes dated July 1910. Thomson, Handwritten Notebook, 1910–68.

34. Minutes of Meeting of the College Committee of the Board of Management of the Edinburgh College of Art, 6 April 1911, *Minutes Book of Meetings of Governors, Edinburgh College of Art*, Book 3, October 1910–July 1911, p.64. Edinburgh College of Art Archive, Centre for Research Collections, the University of Edinburgh.

35. Minutes of Meeting of the College Committee of the Board of Management of the Edinburgh College of Art, 4 June 1912, *Minutes Book of Meetings of Governors, Edinburgh College of Art*, Book 4, October 1911–July 1912, p.98. Edinburgh College of Art Archive, Centre for Research Collections, the University of Edinburgh.

36. *Edinburgh College of Art Annual Report by the Board of Management to the Governors for the Session 1908–1909*, p.15.

37. After the completion of his student training, Thomson rarely dated his work. Later in his career he also sometimes reworked older paintings. As such, many of the dates attributed to his artworks are estimates.

38. For a full list of Thomson's artworks at the RGI annual exhibitions see: *The Royal Glasgow Institute of the Fine Arts 1861–1989: A Dictionary of Exhibitors at the Annual Exhibitions of the Royal Glasgow Institute of the Fine Arts*, compiled by Roger Billcliffe, Volume 4, Q–Z, the Woodend Press, Glasgow, 1990, pp.216–18.

39. *Society of Scottish Artists 21st Annual Exhibition*, Royal Scottish Academy Galleries, Edinburgh, 1914 (exhibition catalogue).

40. Thomson, *Architectural Tour (July 3rd 1909) etc.* Thomson read von Herkomer's lecture transcript *A Certain Phase of Lithography* (1910) in October 1914. He kept a series of notes on his technical progress in etching and lithography between 1914 and 1915, which provide valuable insights into this part of his career.

41. It is possible to trace Thomson's travels during this period through surviving dated sketches.

42. Minutes of Meeting of the Board of Management of the Edinburgh College of Art, 6 October 1914, *Minutes Book of Meetings of Governors, Edinburgh College of Art*, Book 7, October 1914–July 1915, p.5. Edinburgh College of Art Archive, Centre for Research Collections, the University of Edinburgh.

43. Minutes of Meeting of the Board of Management of the Edinburgh College of Art, 11 May 1915, *Minutes Book of Meetings of Governors, Edinburgh College of Art*, Book 7, p.69.

44. Thomson exhibited at the RSA almost every year between 1909 and 1976. The only years he did not participate were 1912, 1918, 1922, 1924 and 1926. For a full list of artworks shown by Thomson at the RSA see: *The Royal Scottish Academy Exhibitors 1826–1990: A Dictionary of Artists and Their Work in the Annual Exhibitions of the Royal Scottish Academy*, ed. Charles Baile de Laperriere, Volume IV, R–Z, 1991, pp.316–19.

45. Minutes of Meeting of the Board of Management of the Edinburgh College of Art, 8 June 1915, *Minutes Book of Meetings of Governors, Edinburgh College of Art*, Book 7, p.79. The war had a devastating impact on the Hislop family. After Walter's death, his elder brother John was mortally wounded at the Battle of Arras in April 1917. Their younger brother Gordon was injured several times in the war, and died prematurely in 1929. For more on Walter's life see: 'Walter Balmer Hislop', *Wikipedia*, https://en.wikipedia.org/wiki/Walter_Balmer_Hislop (accessed 30 October 2023).

46. Adam Bruce Thomson, *Wartime Notes Diary*, April–August 1916, private collection.

47. Letter from Adam Bruce Thomson to D.M. Sutherland, 13 November 1968, private collection.

48. Letter from John Hislop to Adam Bruce Thomson, 24 September 1916, private collection.

49. Peploe, *Adam Bruce Thomson (1885–1976)*, p.7.

50. E.A.T., 'Edinburgh', *The Studio: A Magazine of Fine and Applied Art*, Volume 94, Number 414, September 1927, p.205. This article is accompanied by an illustration of Thomson's pastel drawing *The Valley*.

51. 'Royal Scottish Academy: Fifth Notice', *The Scotsman*, 15 June 1929, p.17. The Scottish Modern Arts Association (SMAA) was founded in 1907. Its principal

purpose was to build an exemplary collection of contemporary Scottish art for the nation, at a time when the National Galleries of Scotland did not acquire work by living artists. For more on the SMAA see: Helen E. Scott, 'Northern Pioneers: The Scottish Modern Arts Association', 2022, *Art UK* website, posted 21 September 2022, https://artuk.org/discover/stories/northern-pioneers-the-scottish-modern-arts-association (accessed 28 September 2023).

52. Macmillan, *Unpublished Manuscript*, p.18.

53. Minutes of Meeting of the Board of Management of the Edinburgh College of Art, 17 July 1919, *Minutes Book of Meetings of Governors, Edinburgh College of Art, Book 10, October 1918–July 1920*, p.75. Edinburgh College of Art Archive, Centre for Research Collections, the University of Edinburgh.

54. *Edinburgh College of Art Annual Report by the Board of Management to the Governors for the Session 1924–1925*, p.13. Edinburgh College of Art Archive, Centre for Research Collections, the University of Edinburgh.

55. For more on the instrumental role Thomson played in Wilson's career see: *William Wilson: Print, Paint, Glass* (8 October–13 November 2022), Royal Scottish Academy of Art and Architecture, Edinburgh, 2022 (exhibition catalogue). For more on Thomson's friendship with Crozier see: Ann Simpson, *William Crozier 1893–1930*, National Galleries of Scotland, Edinburgh, 1995, pp.21–4.

56. For more on the advent of Modernism in Scottish art see: Alice Strang (ed.), *A New Era: Scottish Modern Art 1900–1950* (2 December 2017–10 June 2018), Scottish National Gallery of Modern Art, Edinburgh, 2017 (exhibition catalogue).

57. For more on the history of the SSA and its promotion of international art see: Anne Wishart (ed.), *The Society of Scottish Artists: The First 100 Years*, the Society of Scottish Artists, Edinburgh, 1991.

58. Murdo Macdonald, *Scottish Art*, Thames & Hudson, London and New York, 2000, p.181.

59. 'Old School and New: Second Impressions of Scottish Artists' Work', *The Bulletin*, December 1929.

60. The drypoint etching *The Mill, Norham* (*c.*1926, Fig. 27) is thought to be one of Thomson's last endeavours as a printmaker, though he continued to teach etching at Edinburgh College of Art.

61. Adam Bruce Thomson, *Records of Artwork Sales*, Handwritten Notebooks, 1926–67, private collection.

62. 'Scottish Artists: Society's Gift to Edinburgh Corporation', *The Scotsman*, 9 January 1935, p.12. The painting was simply titled *Edinburgh* when it was exhibited at the SSA.

63. Thomson's parents-in-law owned a house called 'Summerside' on Pentland Avenue in Colinton. In the 1930s the family lived there for an extended period, supporting Jessie's elderly mother, though they retained the flat at Warrender Park Road.

64. *Dorothy Johnstone ARSA 1892–1980: A Memorial Exhibition*, Aberdeen Art Gallery (18 December 1982–15 January 1983); Fine Art Society, Edinburgh (29 January–1 March 1983), 1982, p.19 (exhibition catalogue). Johnstone was a talented artist in her own right, who taught at Edinburgh College of Art between 1914 and 1924. For more on her career see: Alice Strang (ed.), *Modern Scottish Women: Painters & Sculptors 1885–1965* (7 November 2015–26 June 2016), Scottish National Gallery of Modern Art, Edinburgh, 2015, p.60 (exhibition catalogue).

65. Letter from Reverend MacCorquodale to Adam Bruce Thomson, 29 November 1963, private collection.

66. Joanna Soden and Victoria Keller, *William Gillies*, Canongate, Edinburgh, 1998, p.35.

67. *Paintings in Water Colour by A. Bruce Thomson R.S.A.*, the Scottish Gallery (Aitken Dott & Son), Edinburgh, 21 October–2 November 1946 (exhibition catalogue).

68. Thomson began executing Borders landscapes before the First World War. In 1913 he exhibited *Bridge over Tweed, Peeblesshire* at the RSA annual exhibition.

69. The painting had been shown at the 1929 RGI exhibition. See: Thomson, *Records of Artwork Sales*, 1926–67.

70. 'Modernity in the R.S.A. Exhibition', *The Scotsman*, 9 June 1938, p.9.

71. Thomson's first submission was a landscape study entitled *Dumfries Rood Fair* (1912). See: *Society of Scottish Artists 19th Annual Exhibition*, Royal Scottish Academy Galleries, Edinburgh, 1912 (exhibition catalogue). After this, he exhibited with the SSA almost every year until 1955.

72. 'Be Tolerant to Moderns: Artists' Motive of Sincerity', *The Bulletin*, 30 November 1936.

73. David Foggie, 'Paul Klee's Work: A Criticism', *The Scotsman*, 15 December 1934, p.15.

74. Thomson visited the exhibition 'Les Maîtres de l'Art Indépendant 1895–1937' at the Petit Palais in July 1937 and made notes on various artists. See: Thomson, Handwritten Notebook, 1910–68.

75. It was not unusual for artists to be nominated multiple times before successfully joining the RSA due to the multi-stage voting system for membership. For details of Thomson's nominations see: *General Assembly Minute Book of the Royal Scottish Academy of Painting, Sculpture and Architecture*, 24 November 1891–22 May 1940, pp.237–79, Royal Scottish Academy Archive.

76. 'New A.R.S.A.'s', *The Scotsman*, 18 March 1937, p.10.

77. The painting measures 128 x 194cm and still survives in its original setting at 28 Hanover Street. A related series of small preparatory studies were retained by the artist. For more on the formal opening of the building see: 'Edinburgh Savings Bank: New Head Office Opened', *The Scotsman*, 27 August 1940, p.7.

78. The portrait of Mary is reproduced in: 'Society of Scottish Artists', *Daily Record*, 28 November 1936, p.14. The portrait of Ronald is discussed in: 'Royal Scottish Academy: High Quality of This Year's Exhibition: First Notice', *The Scotsman*, 23 April 1937, p.13.

79. A.J.D. Porteous, 'Biographical Sketch: Norman Kemp Smith (1872–1958)', in *The Credibility of Divine Existence: The Collected Papers of Norman Kemp Smith*, ed. A.J.D. Porteous, R.D. MacLennan and G.E. Davie, Macmillan, London, 1967, p.34.

80. Thomson, *Records of Artwork Sales*, Handwritten Notebooks, 1926–67.

81. *Edinburgh College of Art Annual Report by the Board of Management to the Governors for the Session 1939–1940*, p.9. Edinburgh College of Art Archive, Centre for Research Collections, the University of Edinburgh.

82. *Edinburgh College of Art Annual Report by the Board of Management to the Governors for the Session 1940–1941*, p.10. Edinburgh College of Art Archive, Centre for Research Collections, the University of Edinburgh. Many Scottish artists contributed to mural schemes for community and military building projects during the Second World War. For more examples see: Hutchison, W.O., 'Canteen Murals in Scotland', *The Studio: A Magazine of Fine and Applied Art*, Volume 124, Number 594, September 1942, pp.98–101.

83. 'Feeding Centres: Edinburgh Community Scheme: Leith Restaurant Opened', *The Scotsman*, 15 July 1941.

84. Letters from Ronald Thomson to Adam Bruce Thomson, 1941–73, private

collection. Ronald passed away in 1981.

85. 'Artist and Architect', *The Bulletin*, 14 February 1946.

86. T.J. Honeyman, 'Art in Scotland', *The Studio: A Magazine of Fine and Applied Art*, Volume 126, Number 606, September 1943, p.76.

87. For more on the Edinburgh School see: *The Edinburgh School and Wider Circle*, the Scottish Gallery, Edinburgh, 5–26 January 2019 (exhibition catalogue).

88. M.P., 'Scots Artist's Lively Show', October 1946, loose cutting from an unknown newspaper retained by Adam Bruce Thomson, private collection.

89. Gordon, 'Adam Bruce Thomson, R.S.A. Obituary', p.42. For a full list of works included in Thomson's 1946 solo exhibition see: *Paintings in Water Colour by A. Bruce Thomson R.S.A.*

90. For more on the development of watercolour painting in Scotland, and Thomson's role in the RSW, see: Jack Firth, *Scottish Watercolour Painting*, the Ramsay Head Press, Edinburgh, 1979.

91. Lynne Green, *W. Barns-Graham: A Studio Life*, Lund Humphries, Farnham and Burlington, second edition, 2011, p.35.

92. The nickname 'Adam B.' is commonly referenced in secondary texts, and is confirmed in a letter to Thomson from his former student Tom Gourdie. Letter from Tom Gourdie to Adam Bruce Thomson, 2 January 1963, private collection.

93. Minutes of Meeting of the Board of Management of the Edinburgh College of Art, 5 March 1946, *Minutes Book of Meetings of Governors, Edinburgh College of Art*, Book 24, October 1945–September 1947, p.51. Edinburgh College of Art Archive, Centre for Research Collections, the University of Edinburgh. According to College regulations, Beaton was due to retire in 1946, but managed to postpone her departure until 1951.

94. Thomson's appointment to the Board of Management is reported in: *Edinburgh College of Art Annual Report by the Board of Management to the Governors for the Session 1950–1951*, p.7. Edinburgh College of Art Archive, Centre for Research Collections, the University of Edinburgh. His range of responsibilities are described in: *Minutes Book of Meetings of Governors, Edinburgh College of Art*, Book 28, October 1951–September 1952.

95. The John Kinross Memorial Trust was eventually established in 1981. Today, it forms the basis of the RSA John Kinross Scholarship scheme, which enables final-year and postgraduate artists and architects to spend time in Florence developing their practice. See: 'RSA John Kinross Scholarships', *Royal Scottish Academy* website, https://www.royalscottishacademy.org/opportunities/rsa-john-kinross-scholarships/ (accessed 9 October 2023).

96. Letter from William MacTaggart to Adam Bruce Thomson, 29 November 1956, private collection.

97. Thomson's appointment as Honorary President of the Edinburgh Sketching Club is reported in: 'Sketching Club', *The Scotsman*, 29 January 1958. For more on his teaching role in Stornoway see: 'Art by an Expert', *West Coast Advertiser*, 31 August 1951.

98. The approximate dating of these trips is based on corresponding artworks that Thomson exhibited at the Royal Scottish Academy.

99. All members of the RSA are required to submit a sample of their work to the Diploma Collection when they become Academicians. It is not known why Thomson deferred his submission until 1961, 15 years after his election, but such situations are not unprecedented.

100. Thomson, *Records of Artwork Sales*, Handwritten Notebooks, 1926–67.

101. Letter from D.M. Sutherland to Adam Bruce Thomson, 2 January 1963, private collection.

102. A selection of letters from Thomson to Sutherland is now held in the Archives and Manuscripts Collection of the National Library of Scotland (catalogue reference Acc. 6599/9). Other correspondence survives in private collections.

103. For Thomson's reflections on Iona see: Letter from Adam Bruce Thomson to D.M. Sutherland, 5 May 1968, private collection. For comments on his difficulties with painting see: Letter from Adam Bruce Thomson to D.M. Sutherland, 13 November 1968, private collection.

104. Letter from Adam Bruce Thomson to D.M. Sutherland, 11 August 1971, Archives and Manuscripts Collection, National Library of Scotland (Acc. 6599/9).

105. Letter from Adam Bruce Thomson to D.M. Sutherland, 13 November 1968, private collection.

106. Letter from Adam Bruce Thomson to D.M. Sutherland, 8 February 1969, Archives and Manuscripts Collection, National Library of Scotland (Acc. 6599/9).

107. Thomson, *Records of Artwork Sales*, 1926–67.

108. *Adam Bruce Thomson CBE, RSA, PPRSW (20 May–3 June 1967)*, List of Artworks Sold, Douglas & Foulis Gallery, Edinburgh, private collection.

109. Felix McCullough, 'Perfection by Adam Bruce Thomson', *Edinburgh Evening News*, 9 June 1967. McCullough did not seem to realise that this was actually Thomson's third solo exhibition, the artist having staged previous shows at the Scottish Gallery in 1946 and the Scottish Arts Club earlier in 1967.

110. Letter from Adam Bruce Thomson to D.M. Sutherland, 11 June 1967, Archives and Manuscripts Collection, National Library of Scotland (Acc. 6599/9).

111. Letter from Adam Bruce Thomson to William MacTaggart (RSA President), 3 December 1970, Royal Scottish Academy Archive.

112. Letter from Robin Philipson (RSA President) to Adam Bruce Thomson, 12 June 1976, private collection.

113. Edward Gage, 'The 150th: Diversity Brings Its Problems', *The Scotsman*, 3 May 1976.

114. *Order of Proceedings for Edinburgh College of Art Dinner in Honour of Adam Bruce Thomson*, 21 February 1975, private collection.

115. Arthur Melville Clark, *Handwritten Speech Notes for 90th Birthday Dinner for Adam Bruce Thomson*, 1975, Royal Scottish Academy Archive.

116. The centenary exhibition at the Scottish Gallery comprised 96 artworks, including oils, watercolours, pastels, drawings and prints. See: *Adam Bruce Thomson OBE, RSA, HRSW (1885–1976): Paintings from the Artist's Studio – A Centenary Exhibition*, the Scottish Gallery, Edinburgh, 14 January–6 February 1985 (exhibition catalogue).

117. A collection of 24 sketchbooks was donated to the National Library of Scotland in 1981. The copper etching plate for *Edinburgh – Canal Basin* (c.1913) was gifted to the City of Edinburgh's art collection in 1985. Five artworks were presented to the National Galleries of Scotland in 2013. A further self-portrait was donated to the National Galleries of Scotland by the next generation of Thomson's descendants in 2017.

118. Obituaries for Thomson consistently emphasised his considerate nature, kindness and loyalty. See: Edward Gage, 'Adam Bruce Thomson', *The Scotsman*, 6 December 1976. See also: Gordon, 'Adam Bruce Thomson, R.S.A. Obituary', pp.40–44.

119. The author is most grateful to Robin Rodger, Documentation Officer at the Royal Scottish Academy, for drawing attention to this ongoing award.

CATALOGUE OF
WORKS

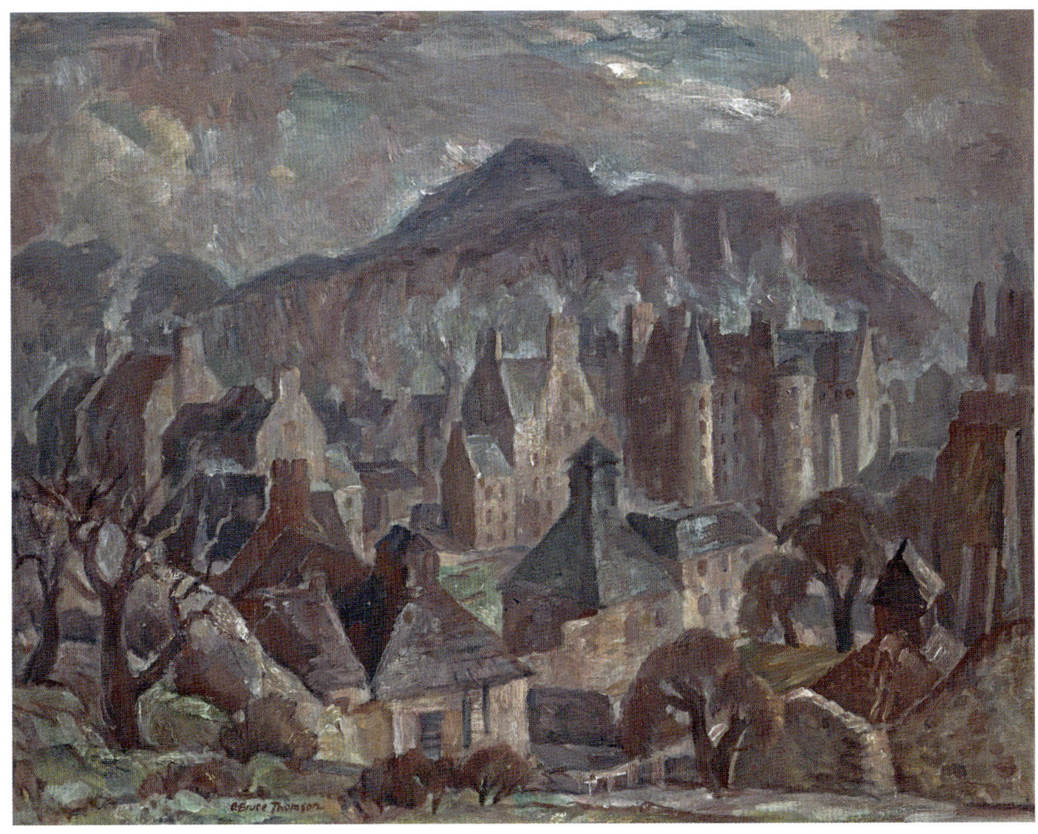

Adam Bruce Thomson, *Edinburgh: Old Town*, c.1951. Private Collection. © The artist's estate.
(Photograph: Antonia Reeve)

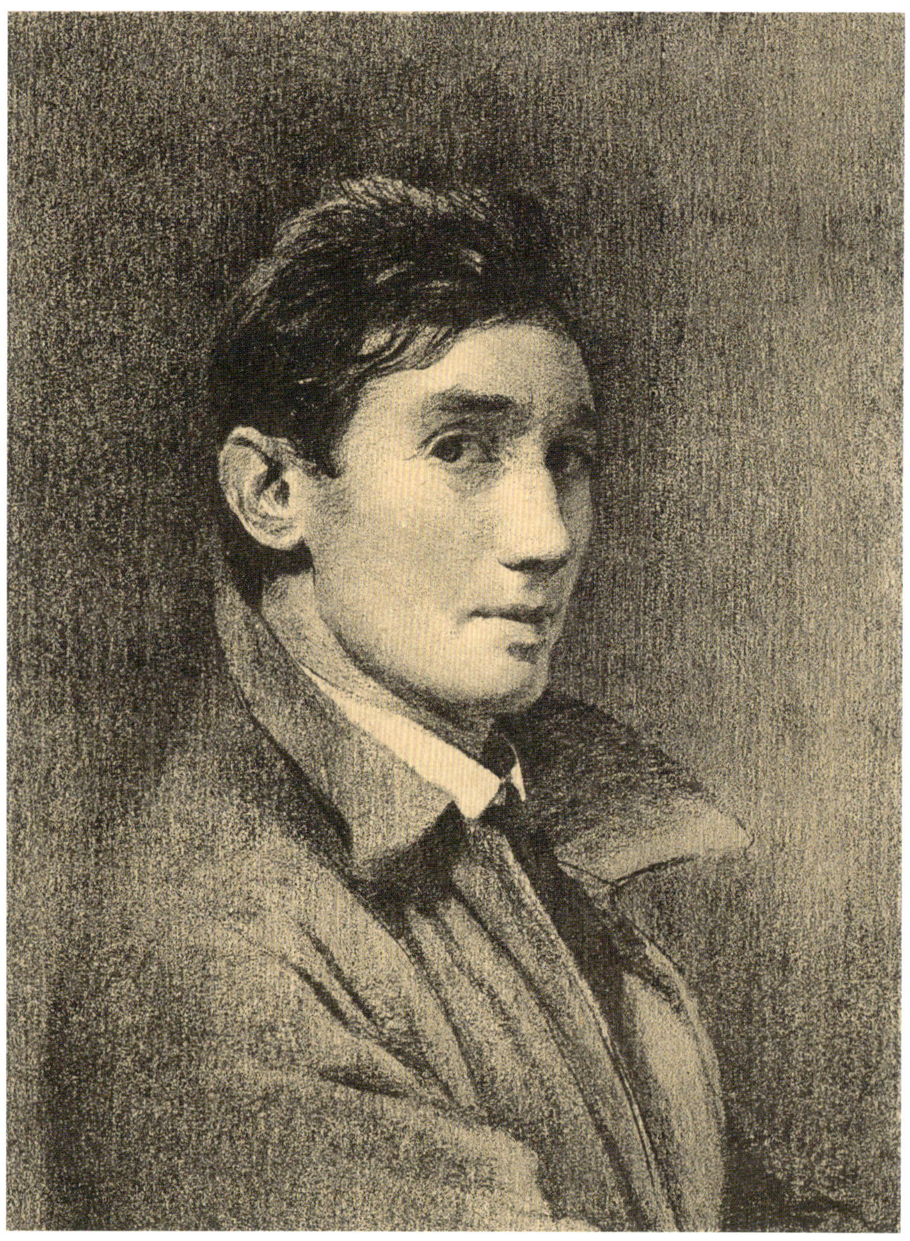

PLATE 1

Self-Portrait
Lithograph on paper, *c*.1910–15, 35 x 25.7cm
Private Collection (Photograph: Antonia Reeve)

Adam Bruce Thomson produced self-portraits at different stages
in his life. This one dates from the beginning of his artistic
career, probably not long after the completion of his training at
Edinburgh College of Art. He went on to become an influential
tutor at the College, teaching there for forty years.

PLATE 2

St John's College, Oxford
Ink and pencil on paper, 1909, 30.5 x 19.2cm
Private Collection (Photograph: Antonia Reeve)

Before Thomson found his vocation as an artist, he aspired
to become an architect. He undertook his architectural
training between 1903 and 1908, and received a Travelling
Scholarship upon graduation. He used this funding to conduct
a four-month tour of southern England, where he made a
series of architectural studies. In Oxford he was particularly
impressed by the university colleges. This precise drawing
records the elaborate east façade of Canterbury Quadrangle in
St John's College.

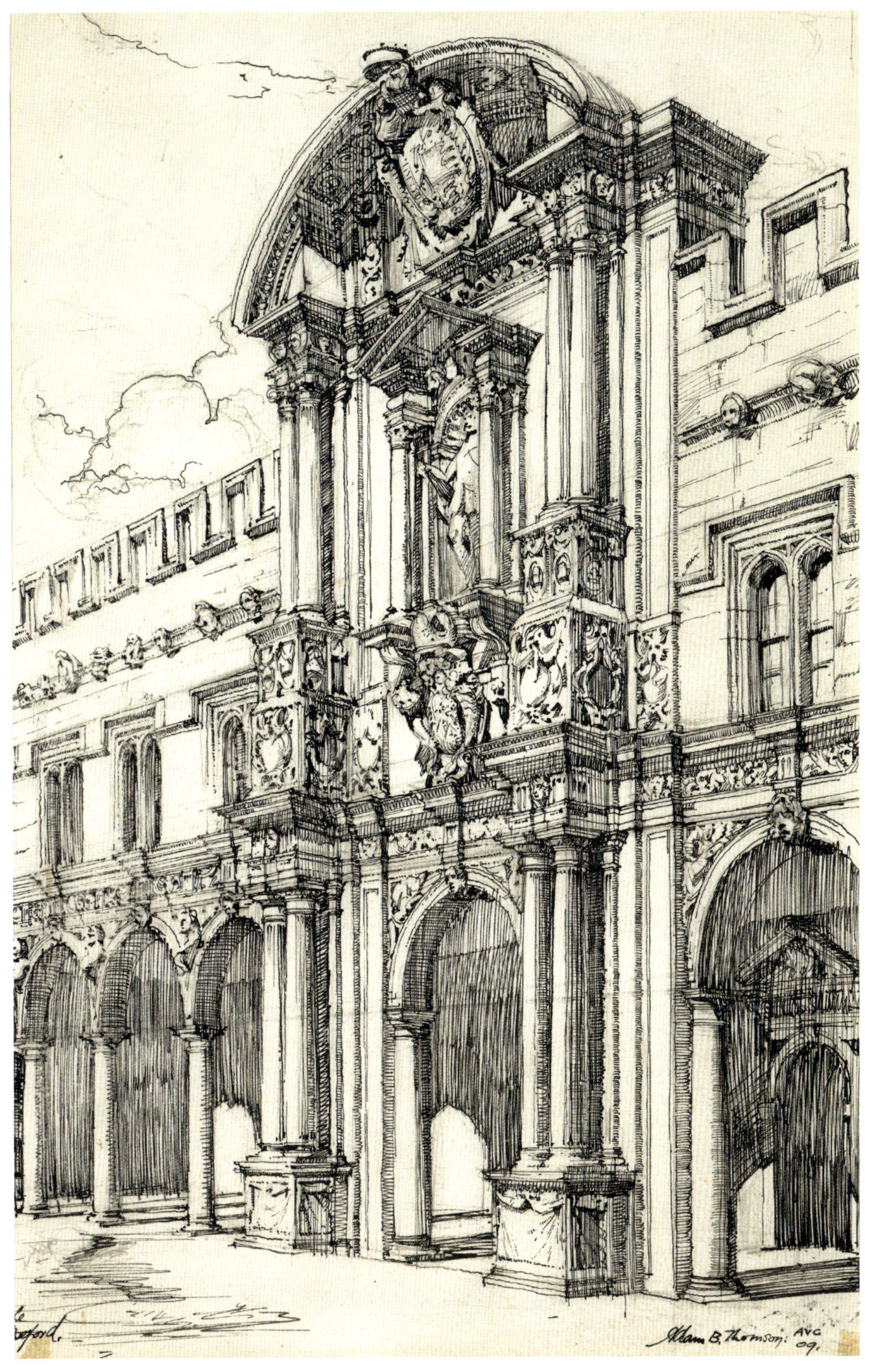

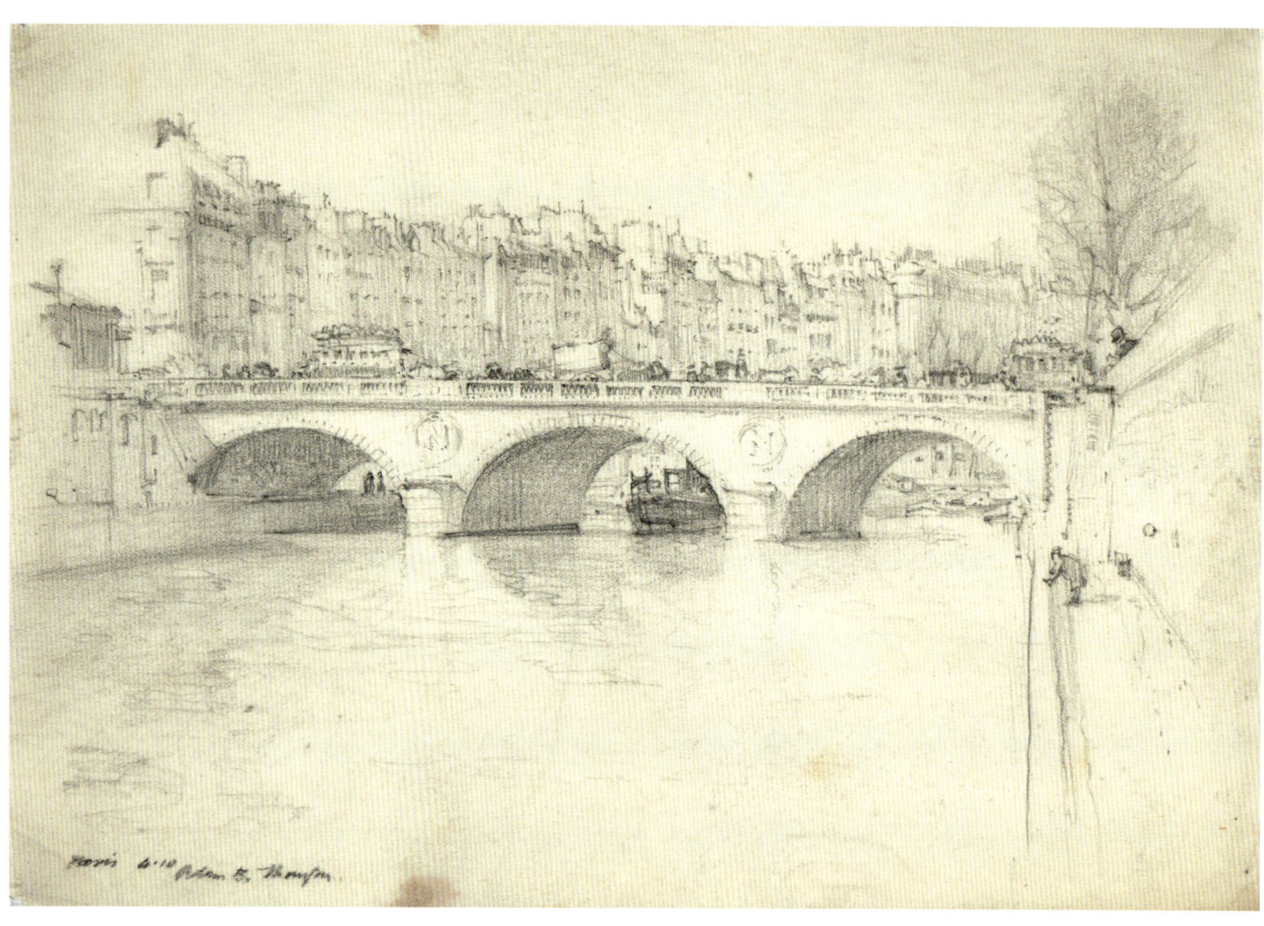

Plate 3

Pont Saint-Michel, Paris
Pencil on paper, 1910, 17.2 x 24.8cm
Private Collection (Photograph: Antonia Reeve)

After finishing his studies in Drawing and Painting, Thomson
received a second Travelling Scholarship, which enabled him
to spend time abroad. This drawing dates from April 1910,
while he was staying in Paris. The French capital offered a
variety of picturesque locations for sketching, as well as world-
class galleries and art collections to visit. His lodgings in the
Latin Quarter were close to Pont Saint-Michel.

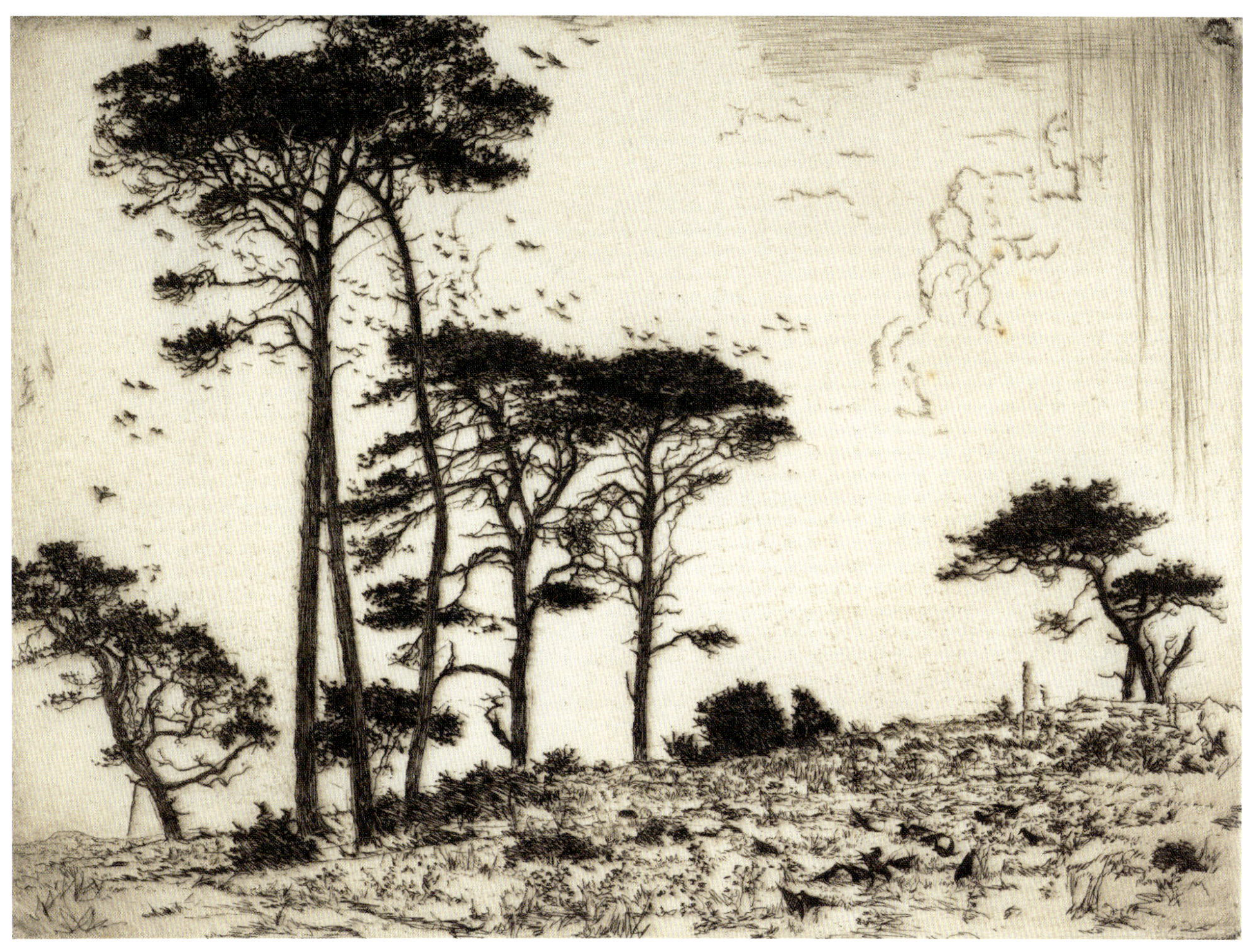

PLATE 4

A Hillside Rookery
Etching on paper, *c.*1910–14, 20.5 x 30.5cm
(plate dimensions 17.5 x 24.3cm)
Private Collection (Photograph: Antonia Reeve)

Prior to the First World War, Thomson's artistic practice focused
on printmaking. He had learned etching techniques as part
of his student training, and continued to hone his skills after his
appointment to the teaching staff at Edinburgh College of Art.
The newly established College had state-of-the art facilities and
dedicated tutors. For several years Thomson taught alongside
Ernest S. Lumsden, who may have influenced his etching style.

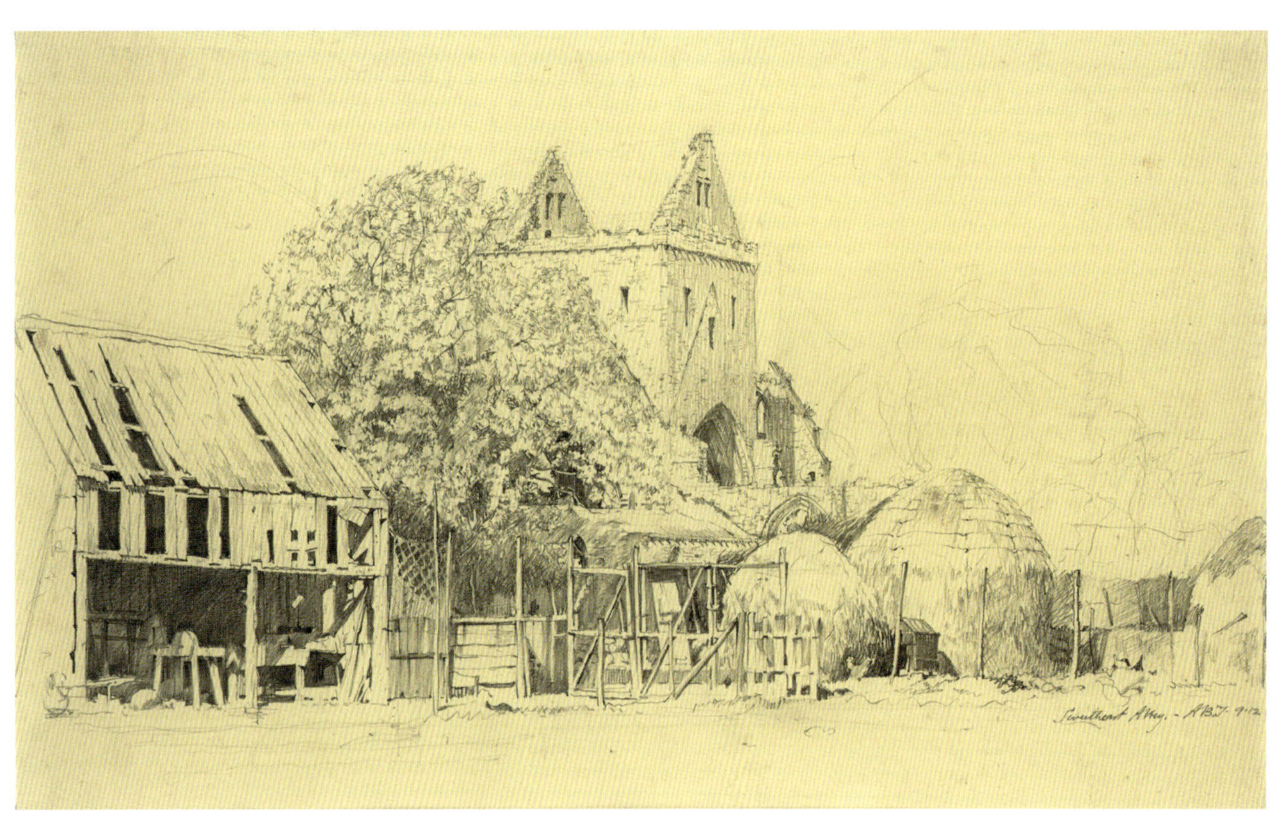

PLATE 5

Sweetheart Abbey
Pencil on paper, 1912
20 x 32.5cm
Private Collection
(Photograph: Antonia Reeve)

This meticulously crafted drawing depicts the ruins of
Sweetheart Abbey in Dumfriesshire, surrounded by rustic
farm sheds and open-air hayricks. Thomson often visited the
Dumfries and Galloway area, portraying rural scenes and
historic architecture amidst the rich countryside.

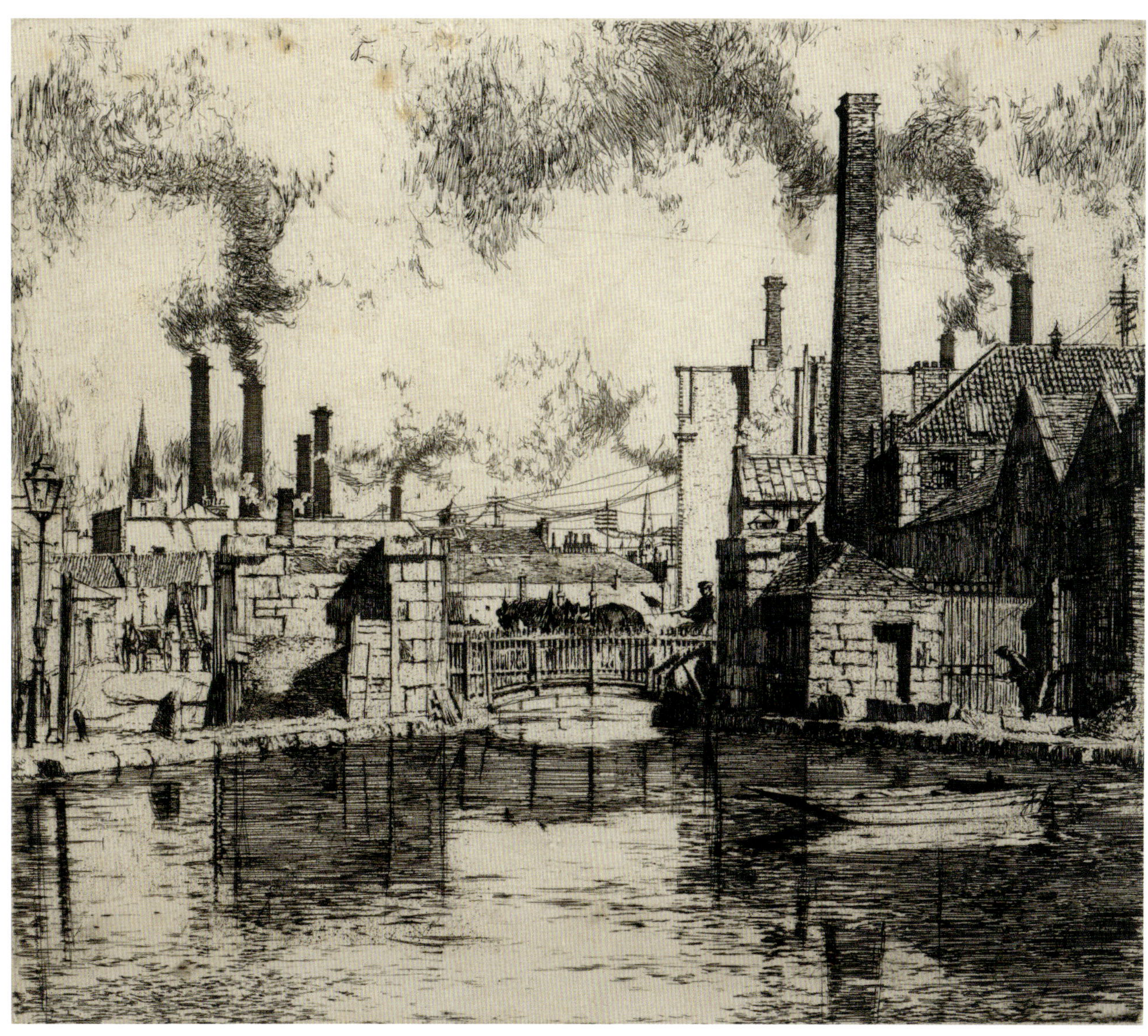

Plate 6

Edinburgh – Canal Basin
Etching on paper, *c*.1913
33.7 x 35.5cm (plate dimensions 19.5 x 22.7cm)
City Art Centre, City of Edinburgh Museums and Galleries
(Photograph: Antonia Reeve)

Thomson addressed both rural and urban subjects in his
etchings. Here, he presents an industrial view of the Union
Canal near Gilmore Place in Edinburgh. The artist would
have known this part of the city well, having grown up in the
adjacent neighbourhood of Dalry.

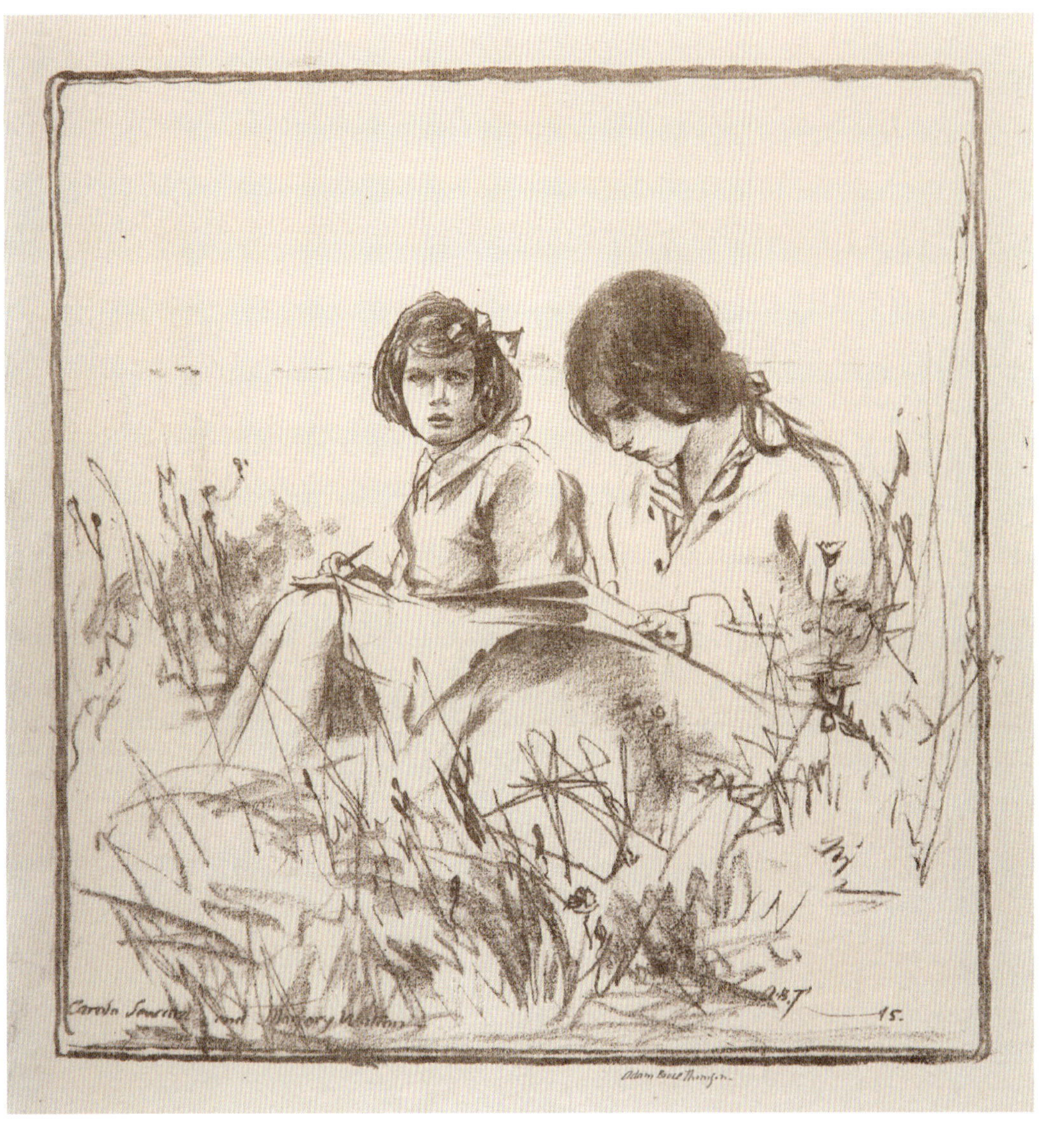

Plate 7

Girls Sketching
Lithograph on paper, 1915
25.5 x 25.5cm
Private Collection
(Photograph: The Scottish Gallery)

Between 1914 and 1915 Thomson kept a notebook documenting his experiments in lithography. *Girls Sketching* dates from this period. The lithographic print is based on a drawing made while visiting the family of the Glasgow artist E.A. Walton (1860–1922). The girl on the right is Walton's youngest daughter Margery. It is possible that Thomson met the family through W.O. Hutchison, a fellow student at Edinburgh College of Art who married Margery in 1918.

Plate 8

Barge on the Thames
Oil on board, *c.*1916, 27 x 29.5cm
Private Collection (Photograph: Antonia Reeve)

As a young man, Thomson stayed in London several times. He sketched from the banks of the Thames and admired the atmospheric depictions of the river by the painter and printmaker James McNeill Whistler (1834–1903). This oil study is related to a series of ink and wash drawings by Thomson showing wartime activity on the Thames. Such works are thought to date from the beginning of his military service.

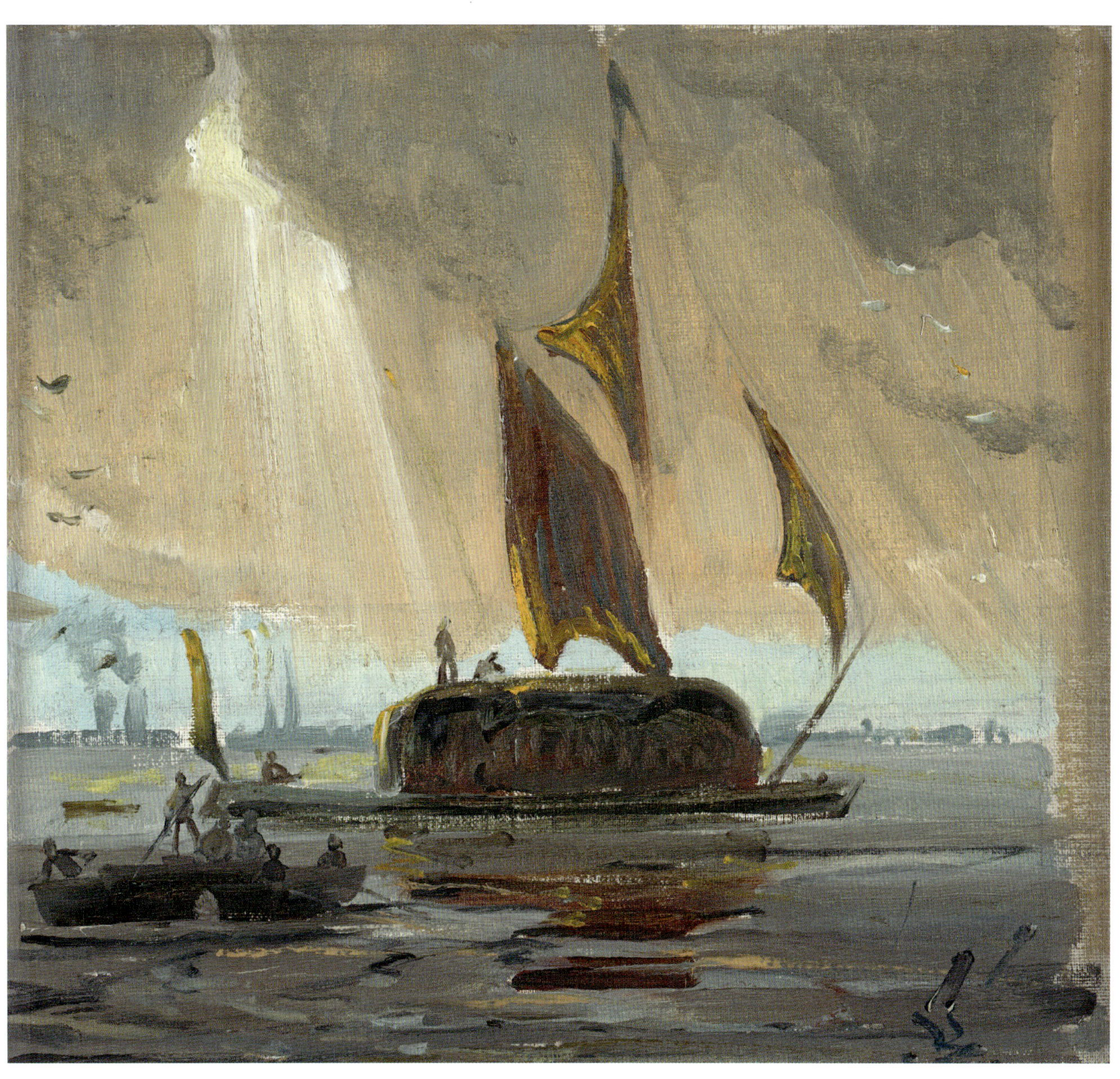

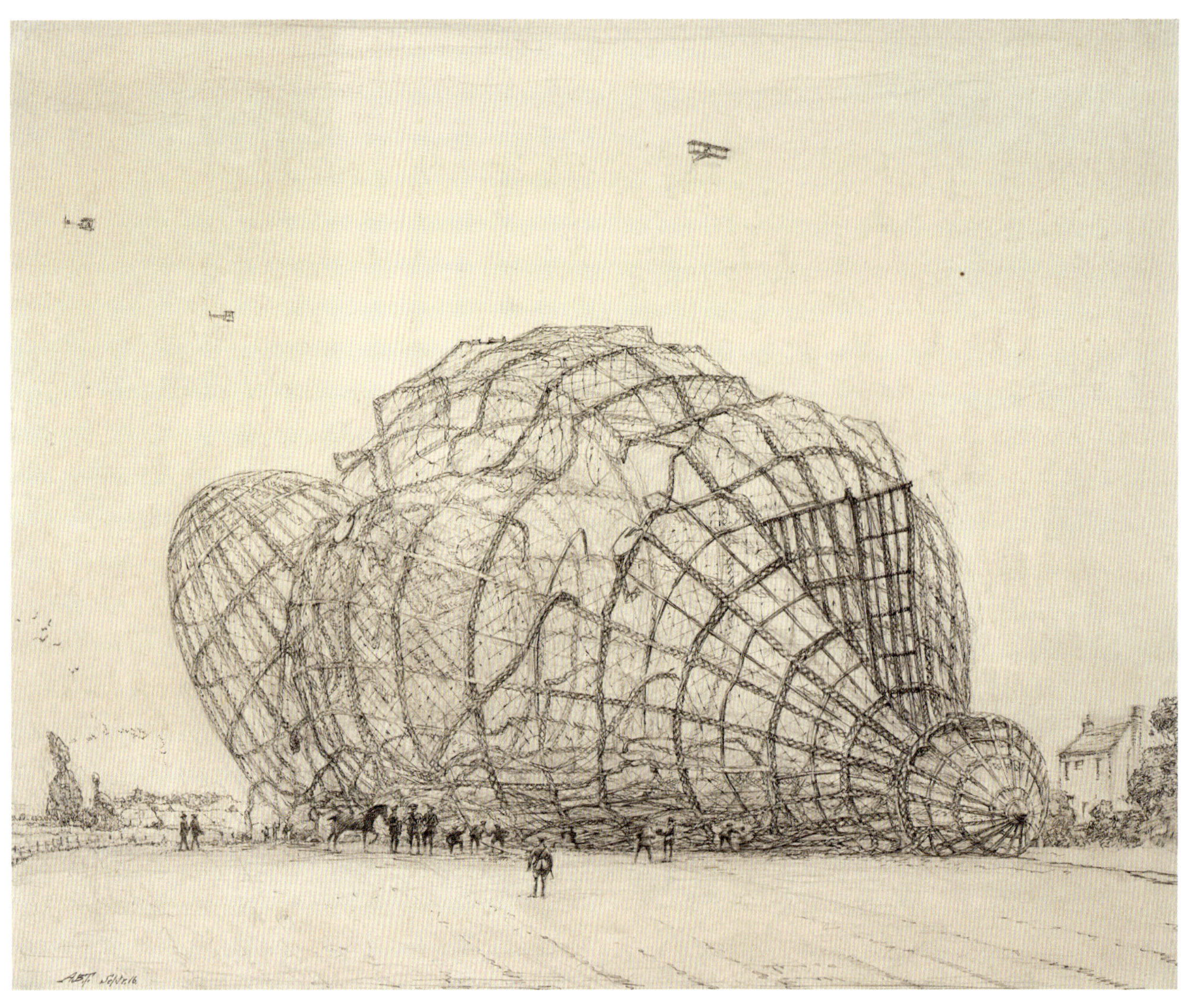

Plate 9

Zeppelin on the Ground
Ink and pencil on paper, 1916
35.2 x 43.2cm
National Galleries of Scotland.
Presented by Margaret Thomson, the artist's daughter, 2013.
(Photograph: National Galleries of Scotland)

On the night of 23 September 1916, a German Zeppelin crash-landed at New Hall Farm near the village of Little Wigborough in Essex. The vessel had been damaged by anti-aircraft fire and attracted many curious onlookers. Thomson, who was stationed at Witham at the time, was among those who viewed the wreckage. He produced this detailed drawing shortly afterwards. According to family and friends, it was executed from memory.

Plate 10

Royal Engineers Building a Bridge near Mons
Lithograph on paper, 1918
21 x 21cm
National Galleries of Scotland.
Presented by Margaret Thomson, the artist's daughter, 2013.
(Photograph: National Galleries of Scotland)

Thomson served with the Royal Engineers during the First World War, overseeing the repair and construction of bridges on the Western Front. After the conflict, he recorded his experiences in a series of increasingly stylised drawings and prints.

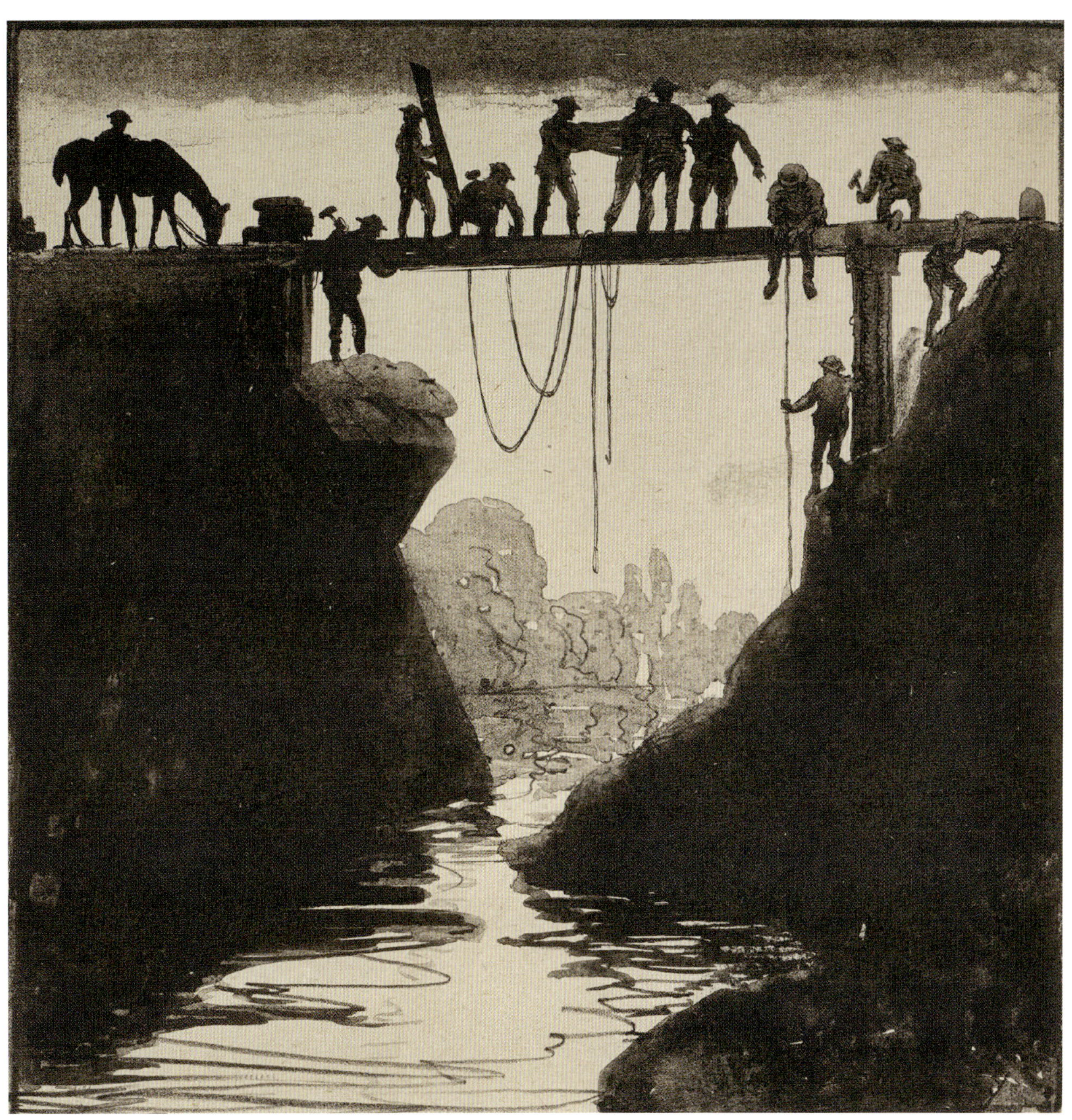

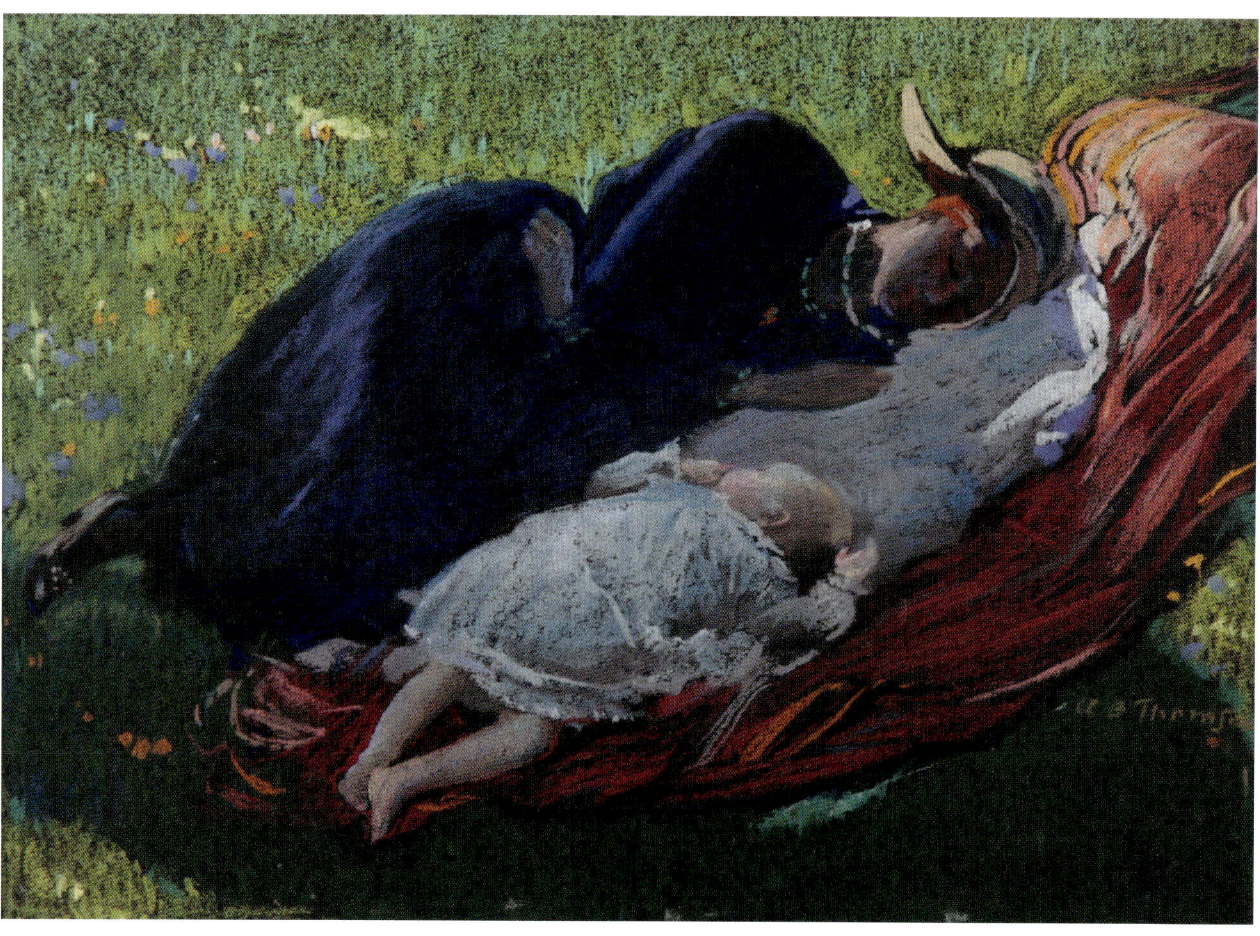

PLATE 11

Young Family
Pastel on paper, *c.*1920–25
25 x 35.5cm
Private Collection
(Photograph: The Scottish Gallery)

Thomson married Jessie Inglis Hislop in April 1918 and started
a family the following year. This intimate pastel study shows
his wife asleep, accompanied by an infant. The artist's three
children, Ronald, Margaret and Mary, feature frequently in his
work of the 1920s and 1930s.

PLATE 12

Beech Trees
Pastel on paper, 1920s
38.5 x 28cm
Private Collection
(Photograph: The Scottish Gallery)

Drawing in pastels gave Thomson a break from the intensive,
time-consuming process of printmaking. He was able to
respond more impulsively to subject-matter and introduce
colour into his work. Here, he uses vivid hues against a
dark background to striking effect. The impact of the image
is heightened by the unusual composition and convincing
suggestion of dappled light filtering through the tree canopy.

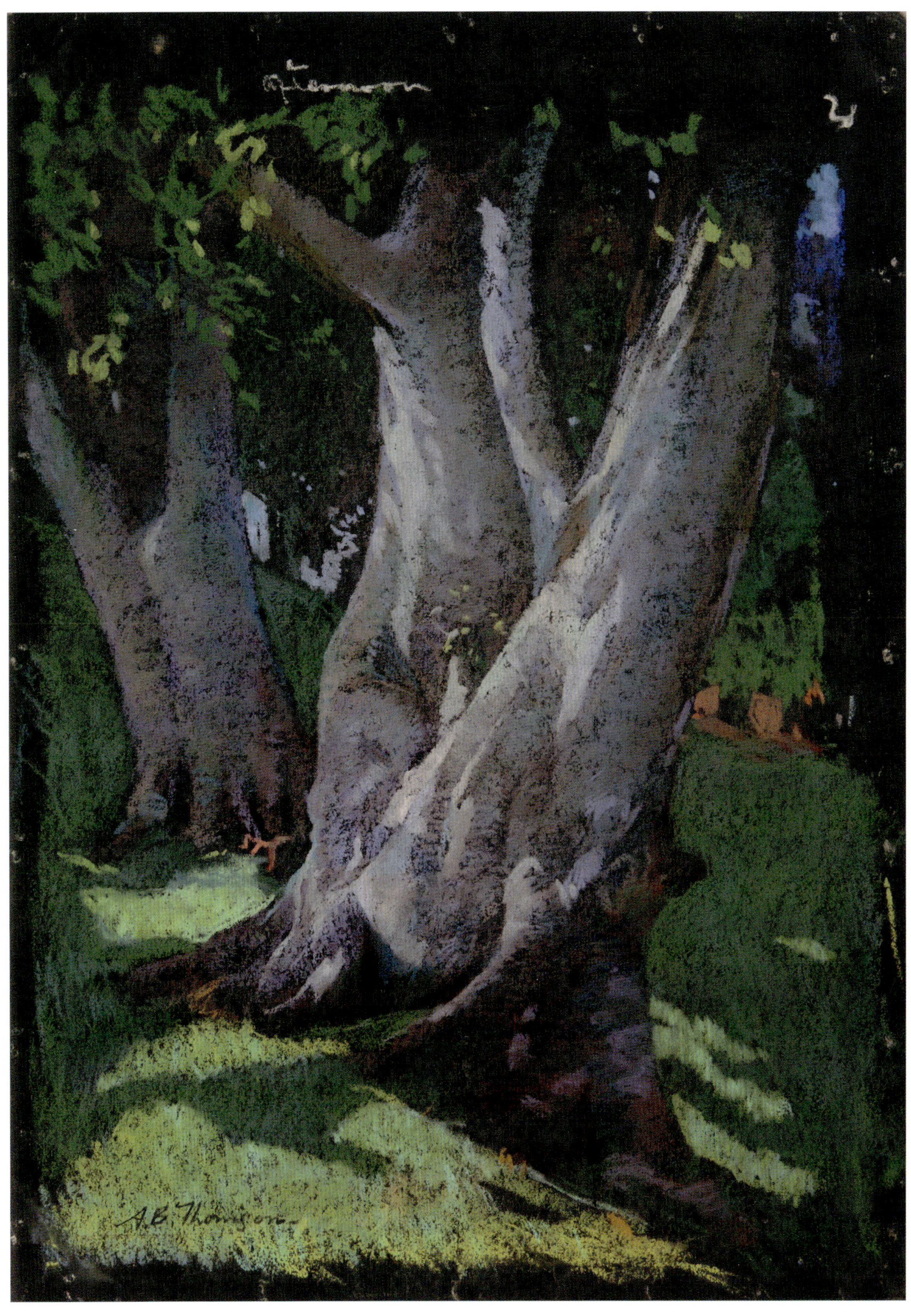

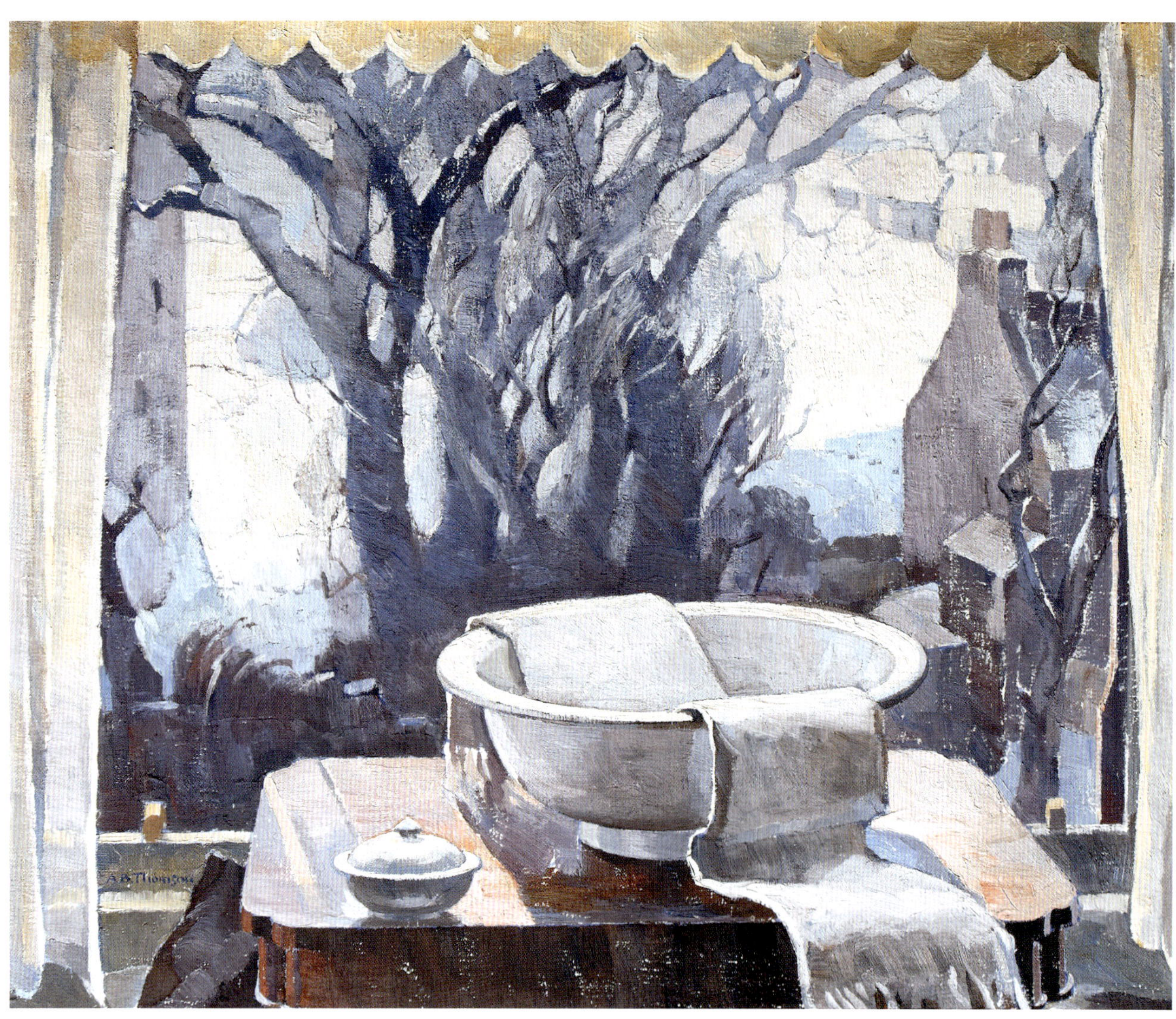

Plate 13

From My Bedroom Window
Oil on canvas, mid-1920s
50.8 x 61cm
City Art Centre, City of Edinburgh Museums and Galleries
(Photograph: City Art Centre)

This carefully structured scene combines the genres of landscape and still life. The outdoor
world is framed by a set of curtains, through which brilliant, white light floods into the interior,
illuminating the washbasin and other items on the table. The elevated setting is the artist's home
at 149 Warrender Park Road, a four-storey tenement in the Marchmont area of Edinburgh.

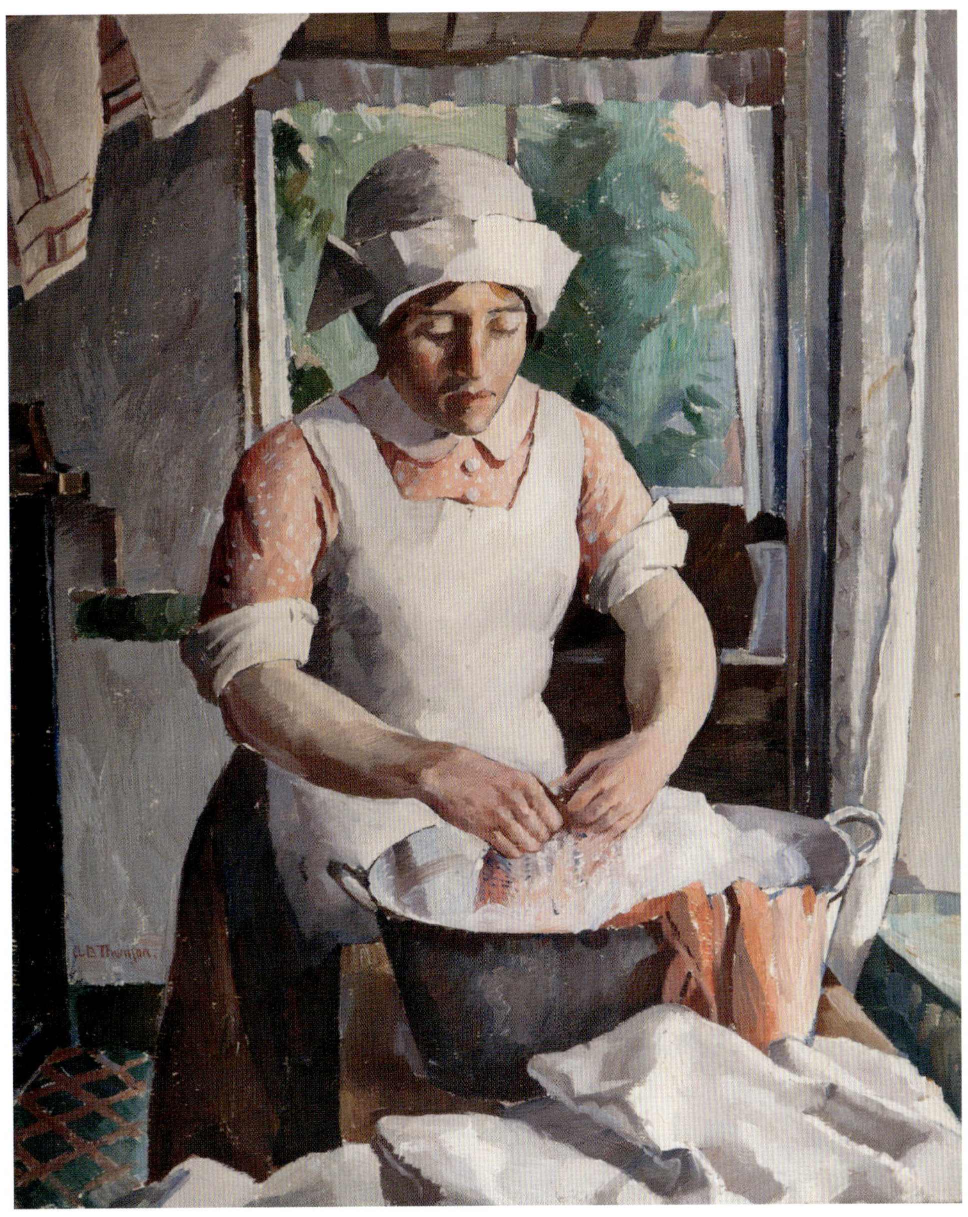

PLATE 14

A Woman Washing Clothes
Oil on panel, mid-1920s
55.9 x 45.7cm
Private Collection
(Photograph: The Scottish Gallery)

Thomson was much occupied by domestic subjects during the
1920s. The model in this painting has not yet been identified,
although her facial features bear a close resemblance to
contemporary portraits of the artist's wife.

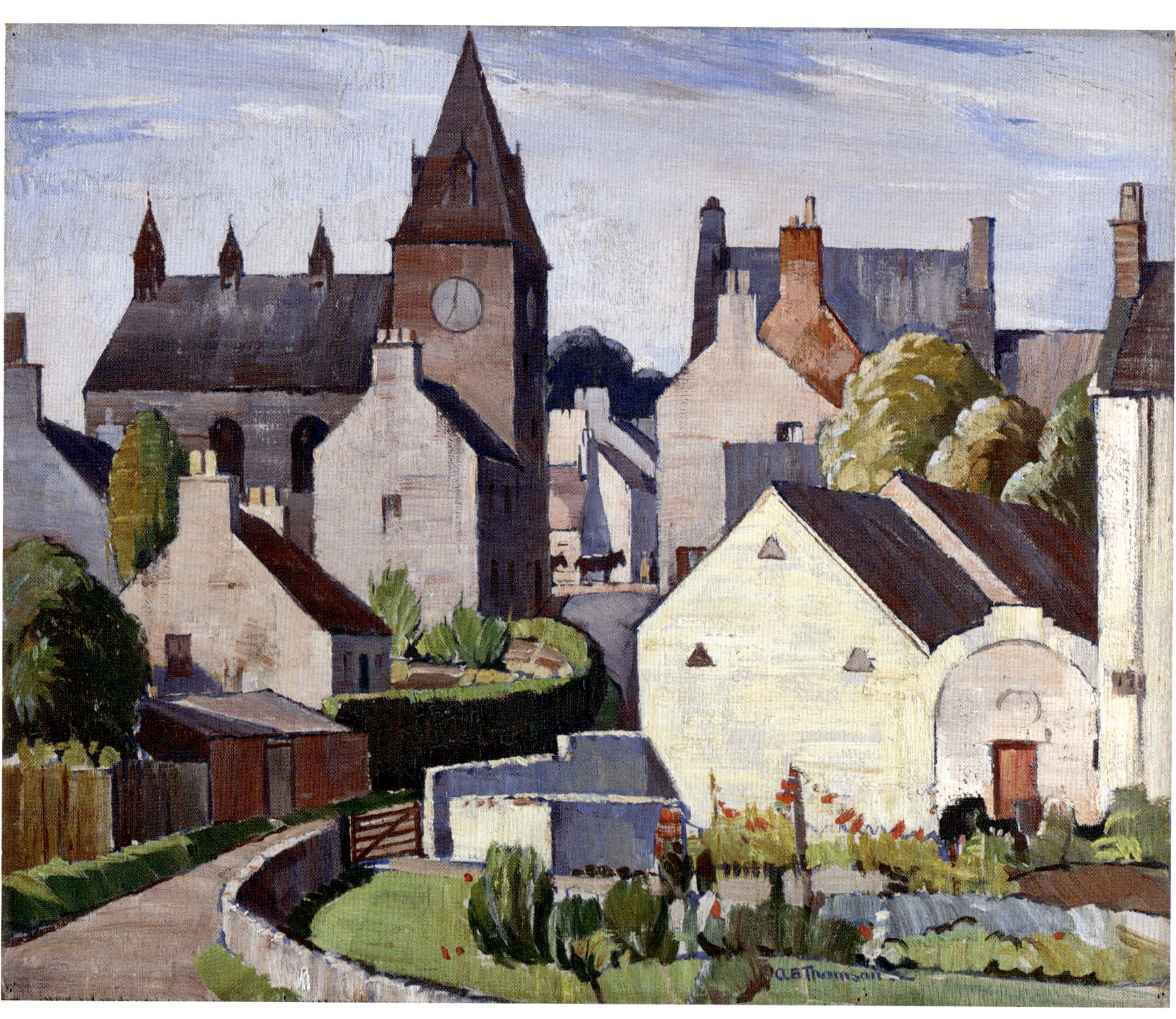

PLATE 15

New Galloway
Oil on panel, *c*.1922–5
46 x 56cm
National Galleries of Scotland.
Presented by Margaret Thomson, the artist's daughter, 2013.
(Photograph: National Galleries of Scotland)

This village scene is thought to be the painting *Gables in New Galloway*, which was exhibited at the Royal Scottish Academy in 1929. At the time, a reviewer for *The Scotsman* described it as 'rudely cubical', making reference to the stylistic influence of Cubism. Thomson never sold this artwork; according to his daughter, it hung for many years in the family's dining room.

PLATE 16

Highland Garden
Oil on board, *c*.1930
76.5 x 63cm
Private Collection
(Photograph: Antonia Reeve)

Thomson was a long-standing member of the Society of Scottish Artists, an organisation which aimed to provide a platform for contemporary art in Scotland. In the early 1930s the Society established a scheme whereby members' artworks would be displayed in local schools. *Highland Garden* was included in this project, with pupils voting it one of their favourite pictures.

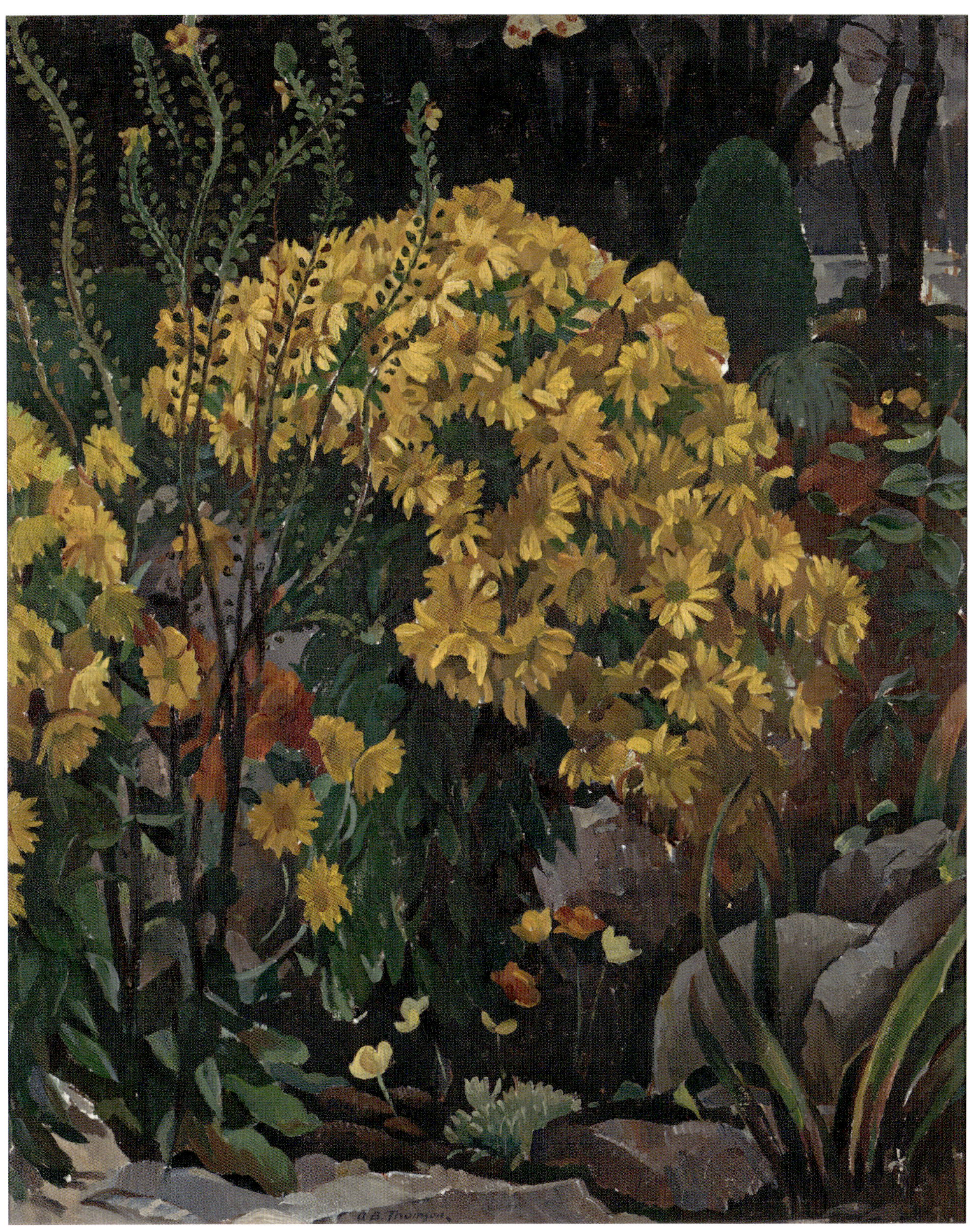

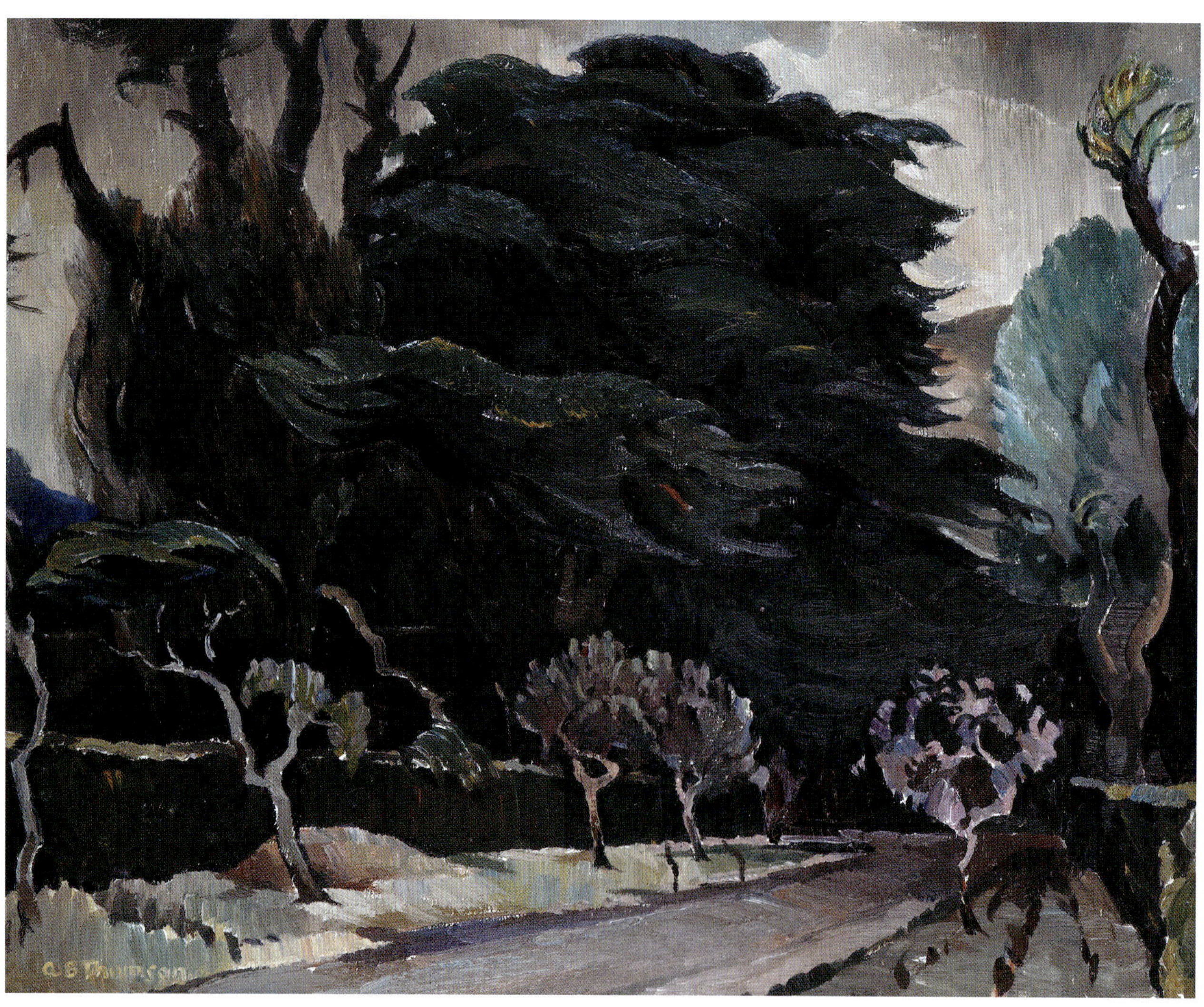

PLATE 17

Cedars
Oil on board, *c.*1931
45.7 x 55.9cm
City Art Centre, City of Edinburgh Museums and Galleries
(Photograph: City Art Centre)

For many years the setting of this moody landscape was
unknown. Recently, new research has uncovered a related
preparatory ink drawing, which confirms the location as the
grounds of Merchiston Castle School in the Colinton area
of Edinburgh.

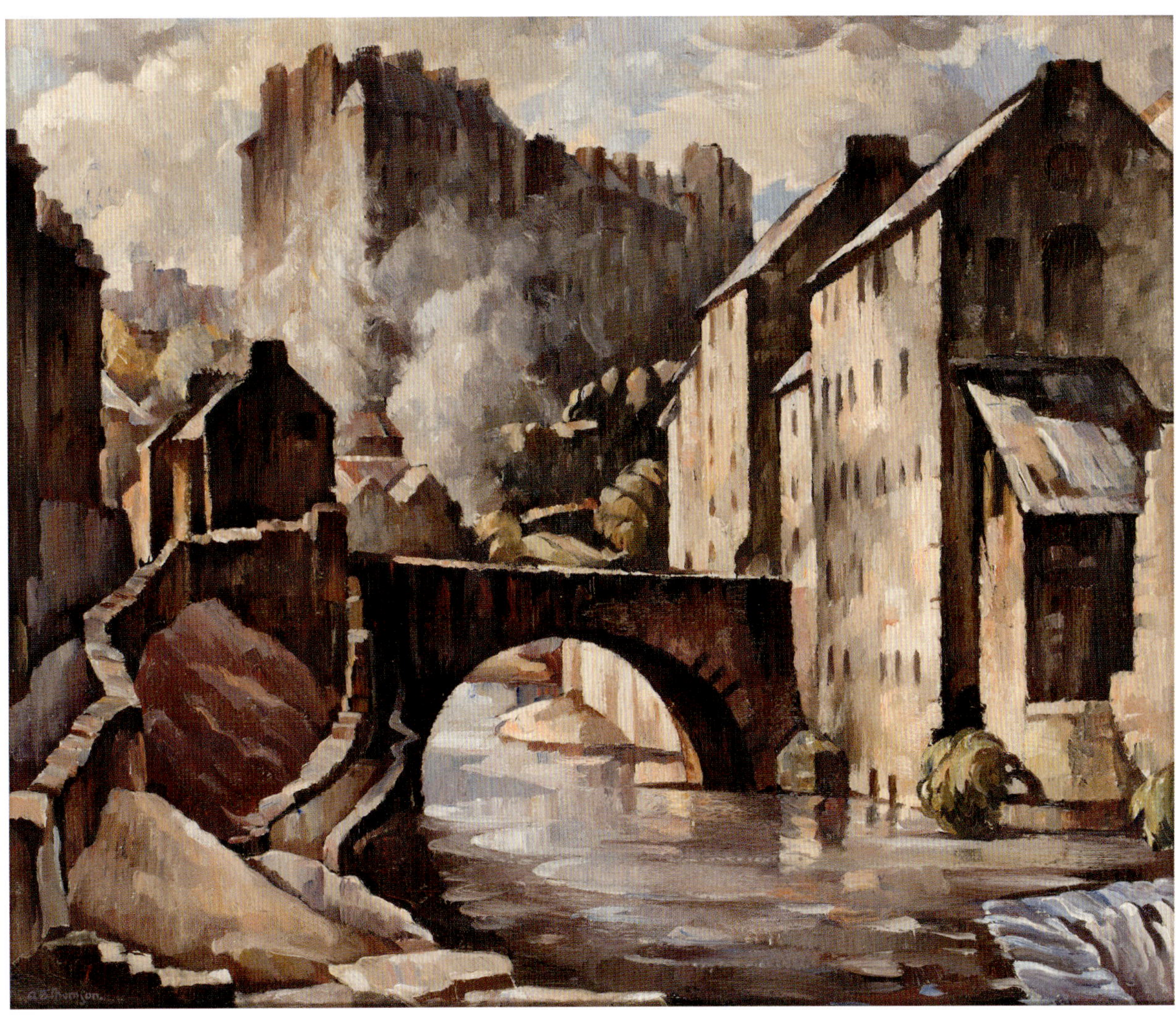

PLATE 18

The Old Dean Bridge
Oil on canvas, *c*.1932
76 x 91cm
Private Collection
(Photograph: Courtesy of Lyon & Turnbull)

Dean Village is a historic settlement to the west of Edinburgh's
city centre, which was once dominated by numerous grain
mills verging the Water of Leith. By the early twentieth century,
local industry had declined and many buildings had fallen into
disrepair. The area was nonetheless popular with artists, who
perceived its scenic potential. Thomson often worked there,
recording architecture on the brink of demolition. Bell's Brae
Bridge, or the Old Dean Bridge, is a structure that still survives.

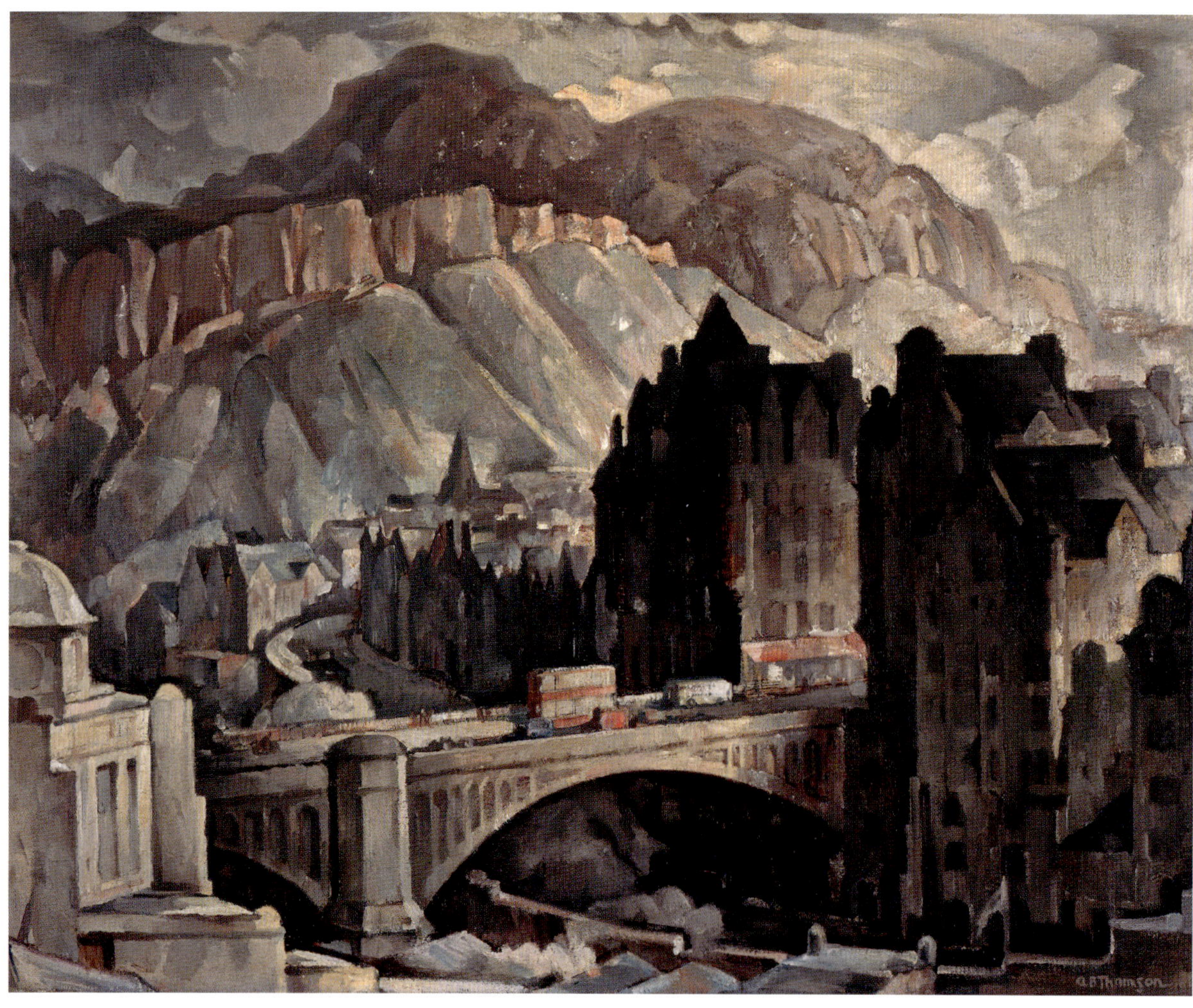

PLATE 19

North Bridge and Salisbury Crags, Edinburgh, from the North West
Oil on canvas, *c.*1934
101.2 x 127.1cm
City Art Centre, City of Edinburgh Museums and Galleries
(Photograph: City Art Centre)

This canvas is the largest-known easel painting from a series
of monumental Edinburgh views executed by Thomson in the
1930s. It received extensive press coverage when it went on
display at the 1934 Society of Scottish Artists exhibition and was
subsequently gifted to the City of Edinburgh. Such recognition
may have contributed to Thomson later receiving a commission
to create another sweeping Old Town scene for the Edinburgh
Savings Bank.

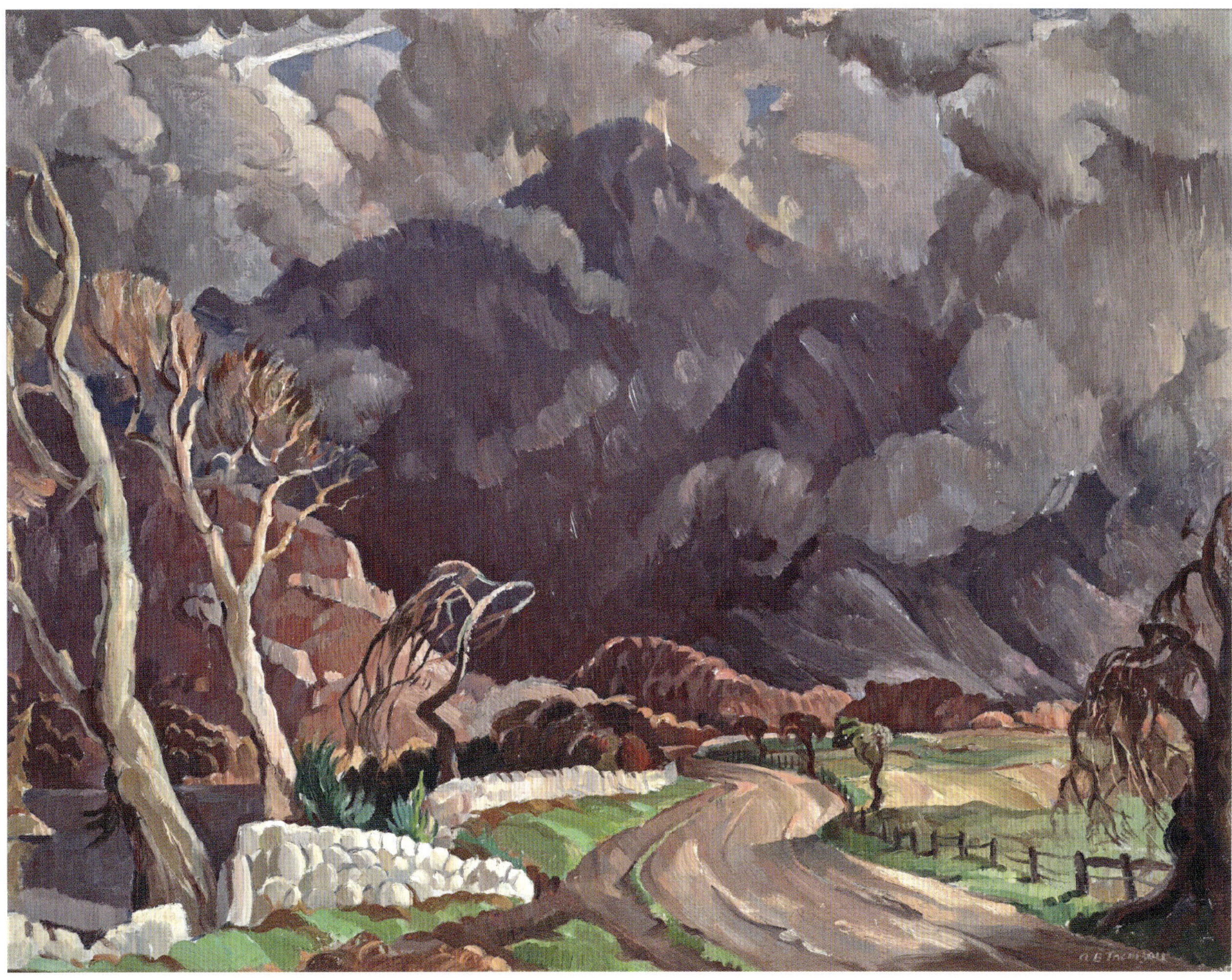

PLATE 20

The Road to Ben Cruachan
Oil on canvas, *c*.1932
87 x 112cm
Private Collection
(Photograph: Antonia Reeve)

The mountain Ben Cruachan stands a few miles from the
village of Taynuilt in North Argyll. In the 1930s Thomson spent
family holidays in the area with the artists D.M. Sutherland
and Dorothy Johnstone. This evocative landscape captures the
notoriously changeable west-coast weather – strong sunlight
illuminates the foreground, while menacing clouds loom in
the distance.

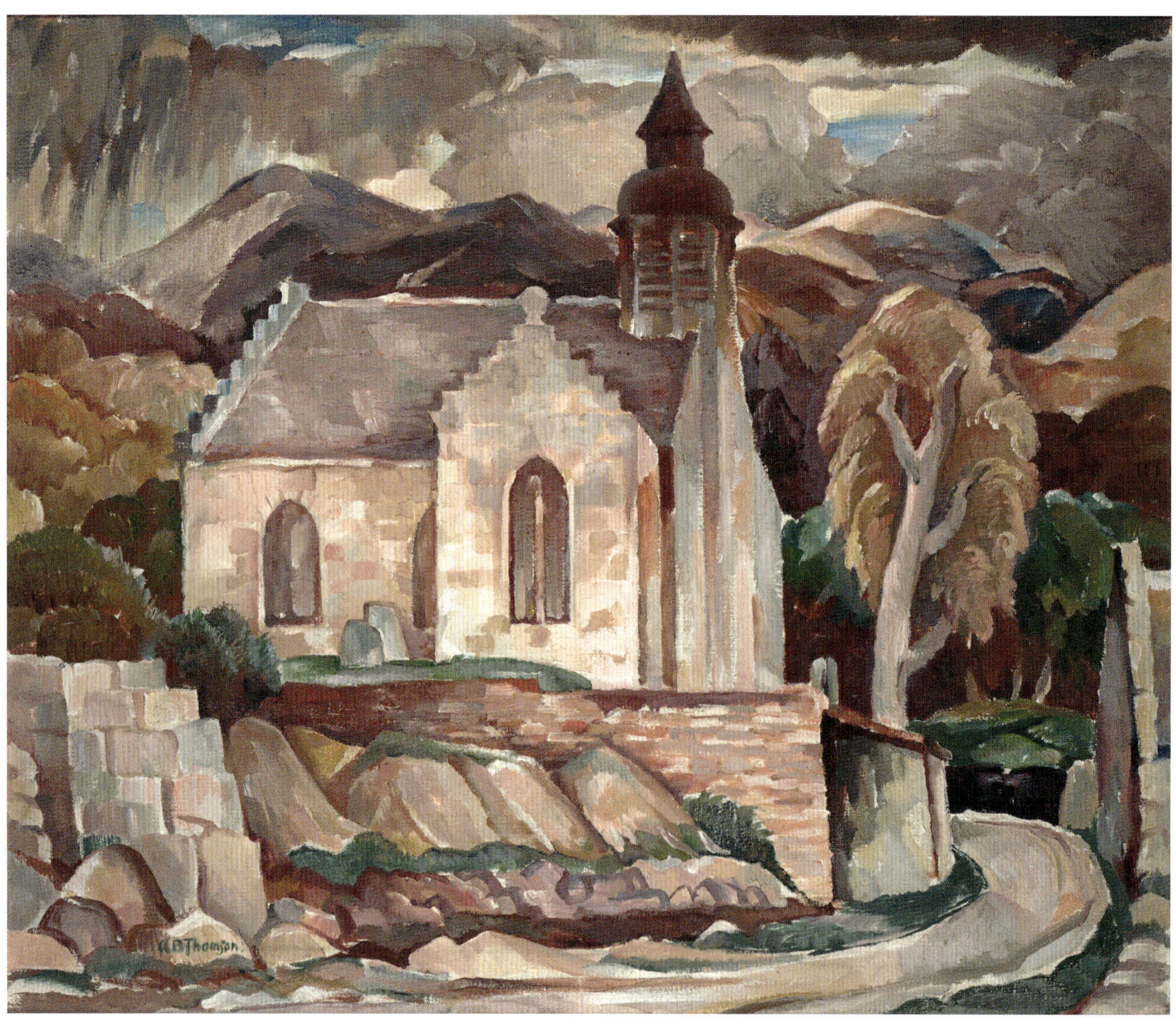

PLATE 21

Achnaba
Oil on canvas, 1930s
77 x 91.5cm
Private Collection
(Photograph: Antonia Reeve)

Although Thomson was primarily drawn to Argyll and the
Highlands for their wild natural landscapes, he was also
interested in the local architecture. Here, he depicts Ardchattan
Church in Achnaba. He painted this distinctive building a
number of times, presenting it from different angles.

PLATE 22

Mary
Oil on linen laid on board, 1936
92.3 x 76.5cm
Private Collection
(Photograph: Antonia Reeve)

Thomson's youngest daughter Mary modelled regularly for
her father's paintings. In this portrait she adopts a casual pose,
curled up barefoot in an armchair. Once again, interior and
exterior scenes are combined in this composition; a rural view of
trees and houses is visible through the window beyond.

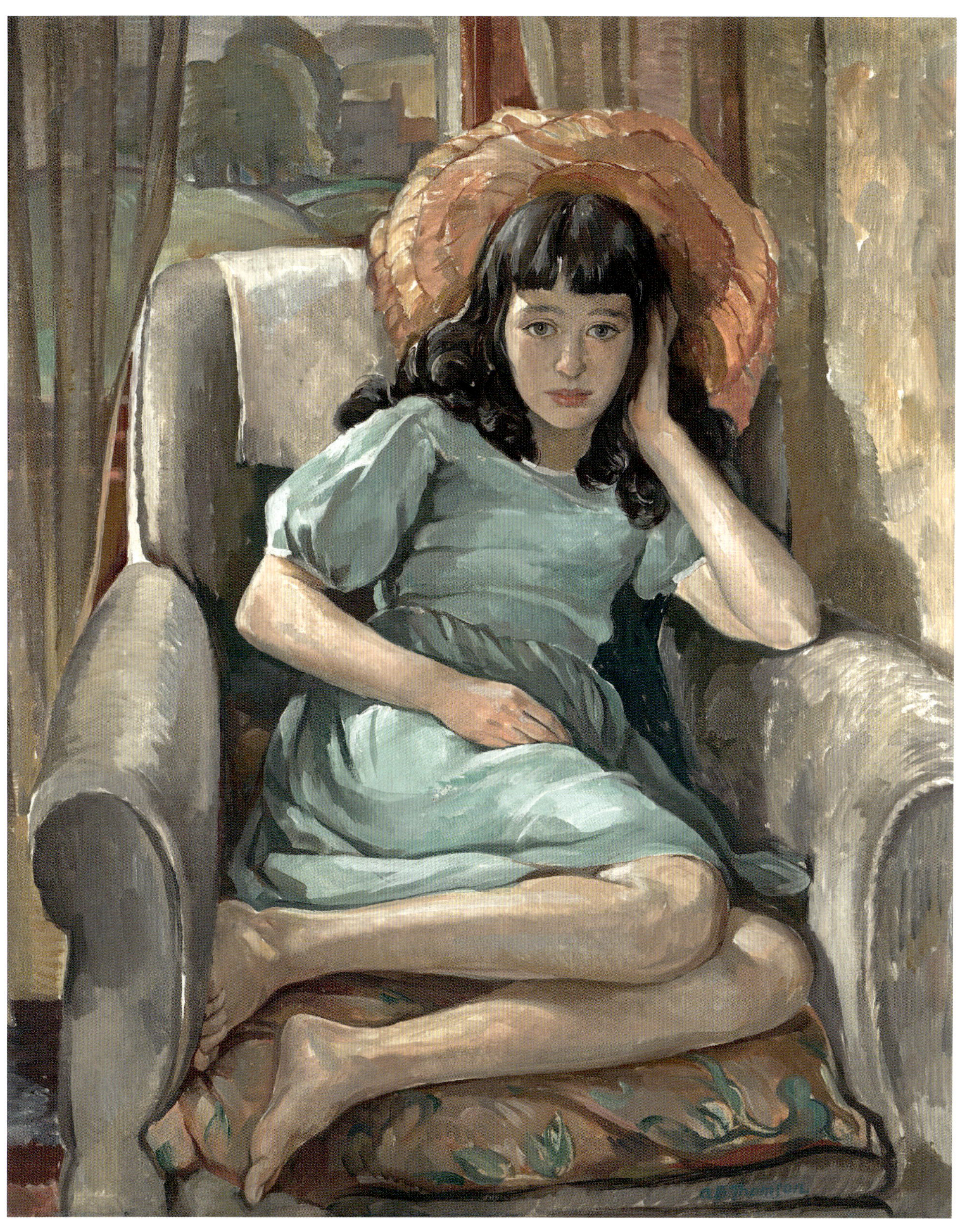

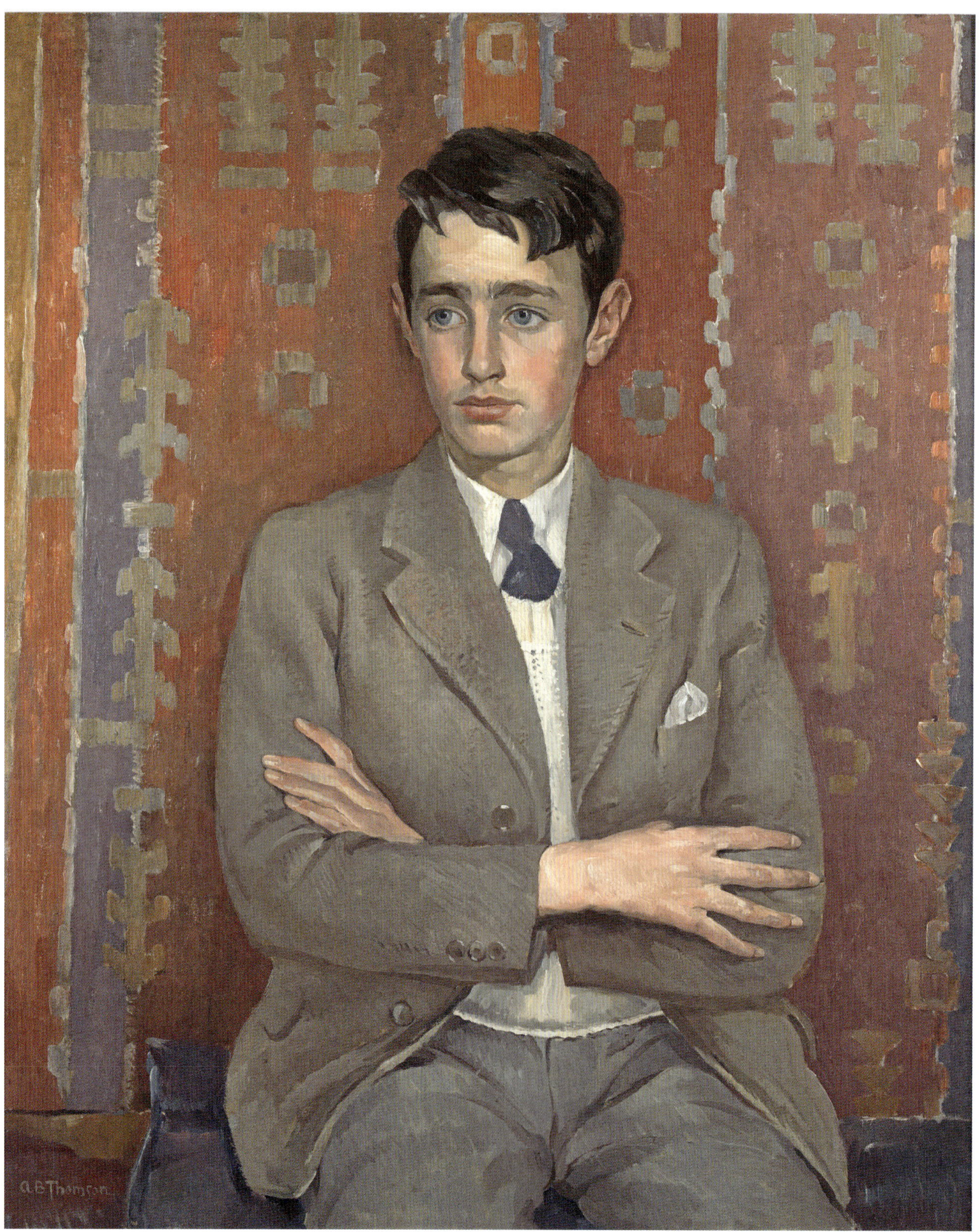

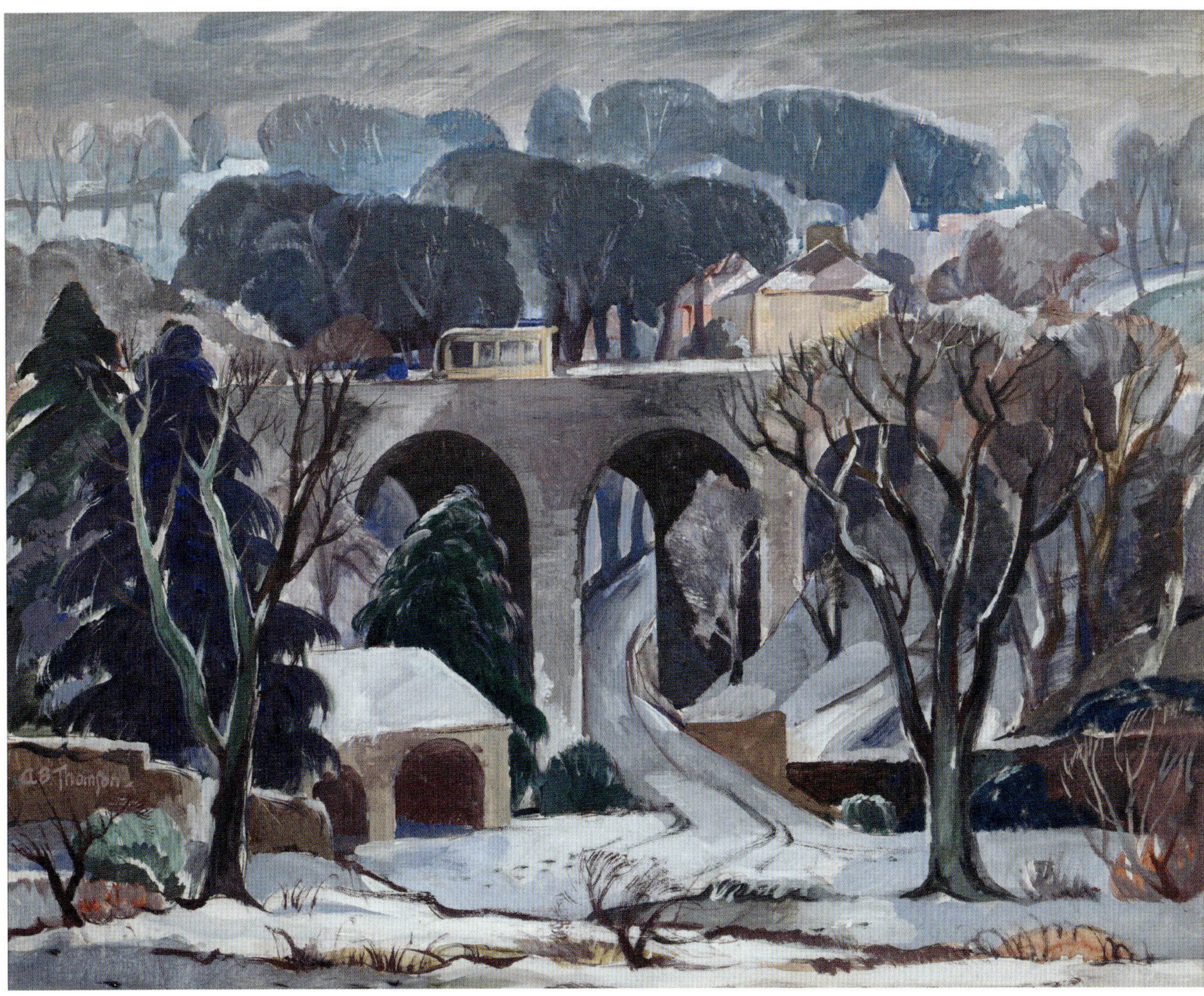

PLATE 23

Ronald
Oil on canvas, *c.*1937
92 x 77cm
Private Collection
(Photograph: Antonia Reeve)

This studio portrait presents the artist's teenage son, Ronald,
before a colourful geometric backdrop. Ronald, known to the
family as Ronnie, demonstrated artistic talents from an early
age. He enrolled at art school in the late 1930s, but the outbreak
of the Second World War and subsequent mental illness
prevented him from pursuing this career path further.

PLATE 24

Colinton Bridge – The Valley in Snow
Tempera on paper, *c.*1937
50.3 x 63.5cm
City Art Centre, City of Edinburgh Museums and Galleries
(Photograph: Antonia Reeve)

Thomson was very familiar with the Edinburgh suburb of
Colinton. His wife's parents lived in the area, and the family
stayed there for several years during the 1930s. This winter
scene centres on the Colinton New Bridge Viaduct, spanning
the Water of Leith Valley, as viewed from the vicinity of
Gillespie Road.

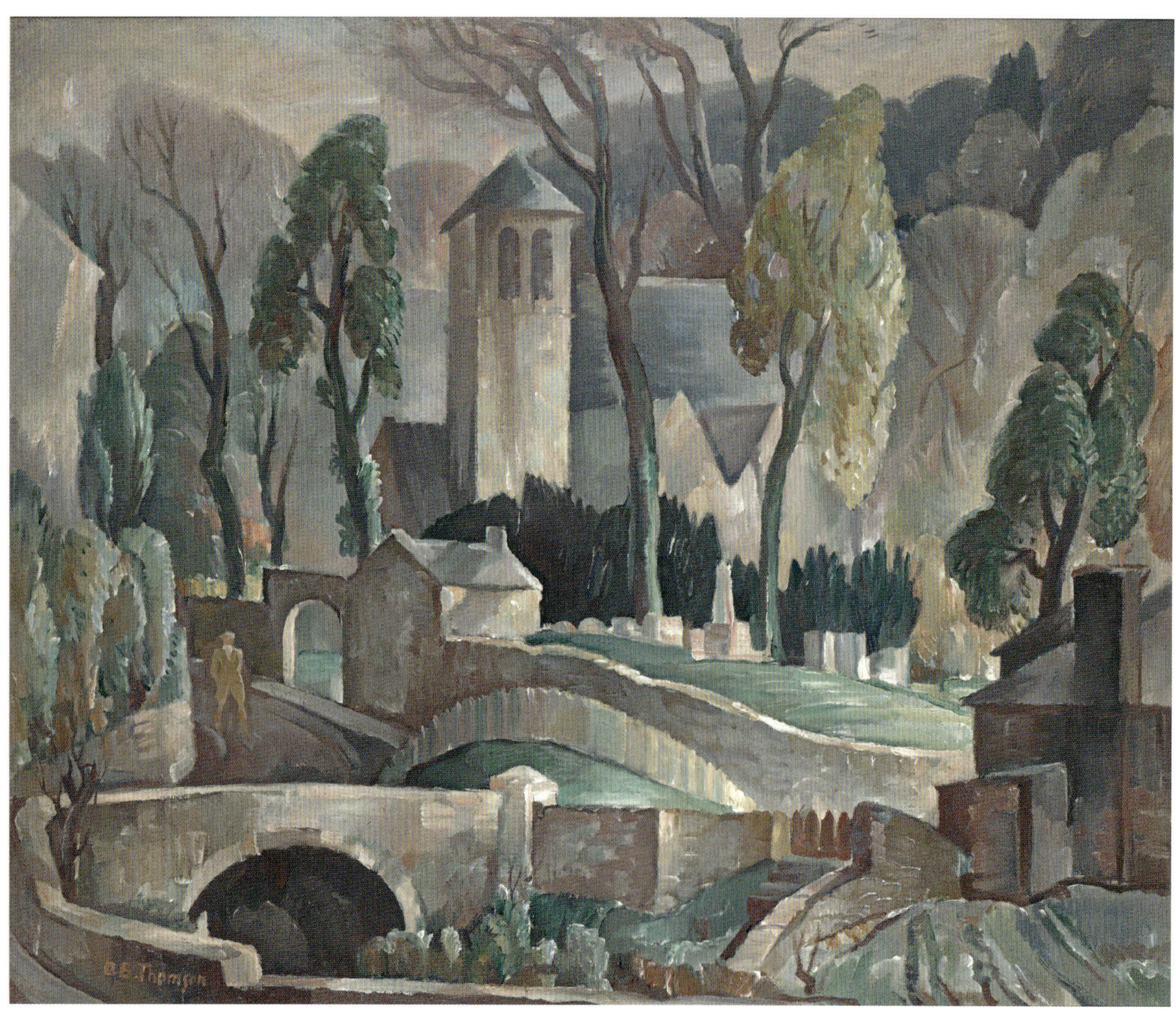

Plate 25

At Colinton
Oil on canvas, *c*.1937
76 x 91.5cm
Private Collection
(Photograph: Antonia Reeve)

Over the years, Thomson painted Colinton Parish Church many
times. His close friend William Wilson was also inspired by
this location, and later designed a suite of three stained-glass
windows for the church.

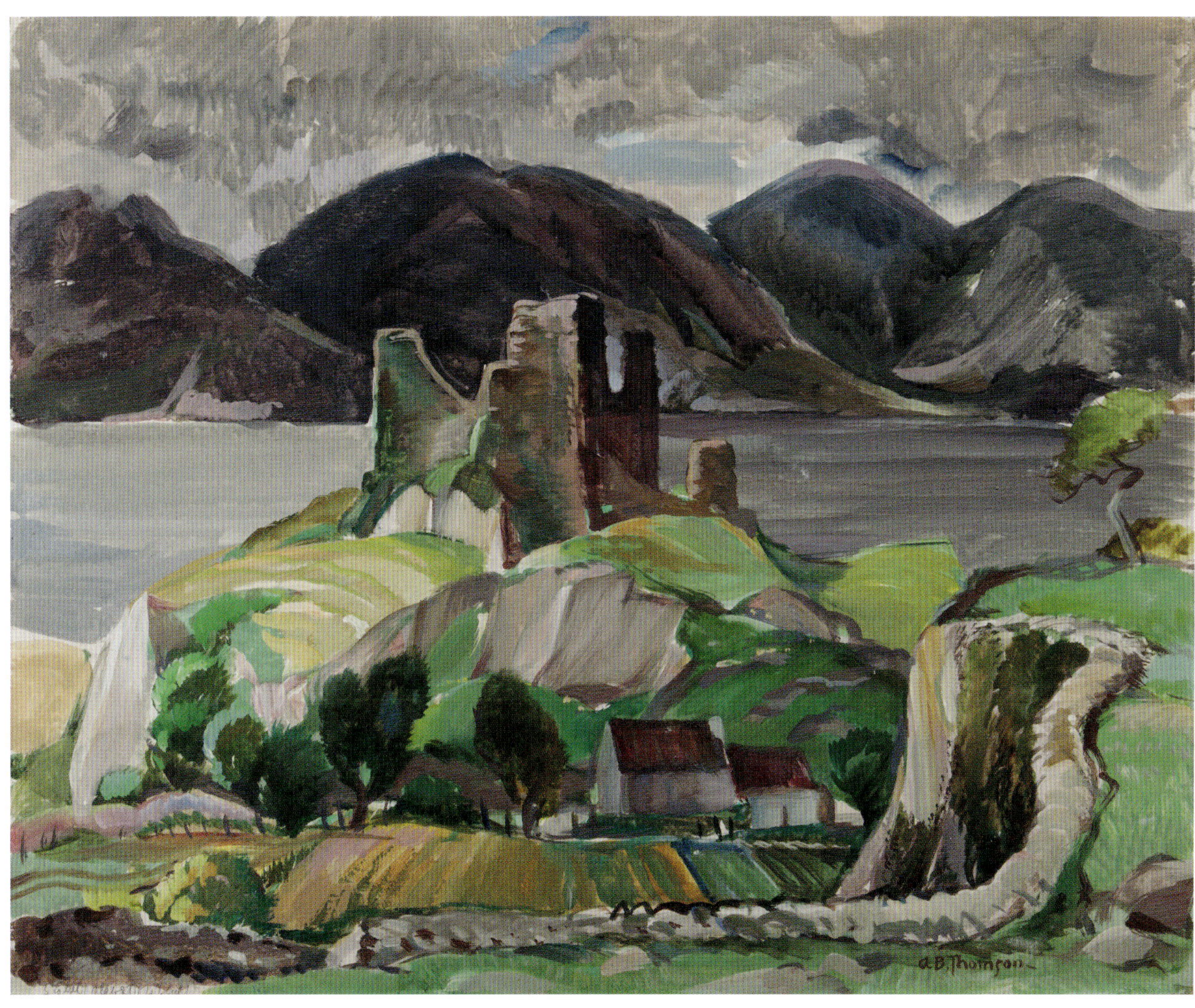

Plate 26

Ancient Clan Stronghold, Castle Coeffin, Isle of Lismore
Gouache, tempera and watercolour on paper, *c.*1937–8
51 x 63.5cm
Private Collection
(Photograph: The Scottish Gallery)

Thomson and his family spent the summers of 1937 and 1938
on Lismore in the Inner Hebrides. His passion for history and
archaeology led him to Castle Coeffin, a thirteenth-century
ruin on the west coast of the island. He made various studies
of this striking landmark, sometimes experimenting with the
ancient technique of tempera painting to achieve a smooth,
opaque finish.

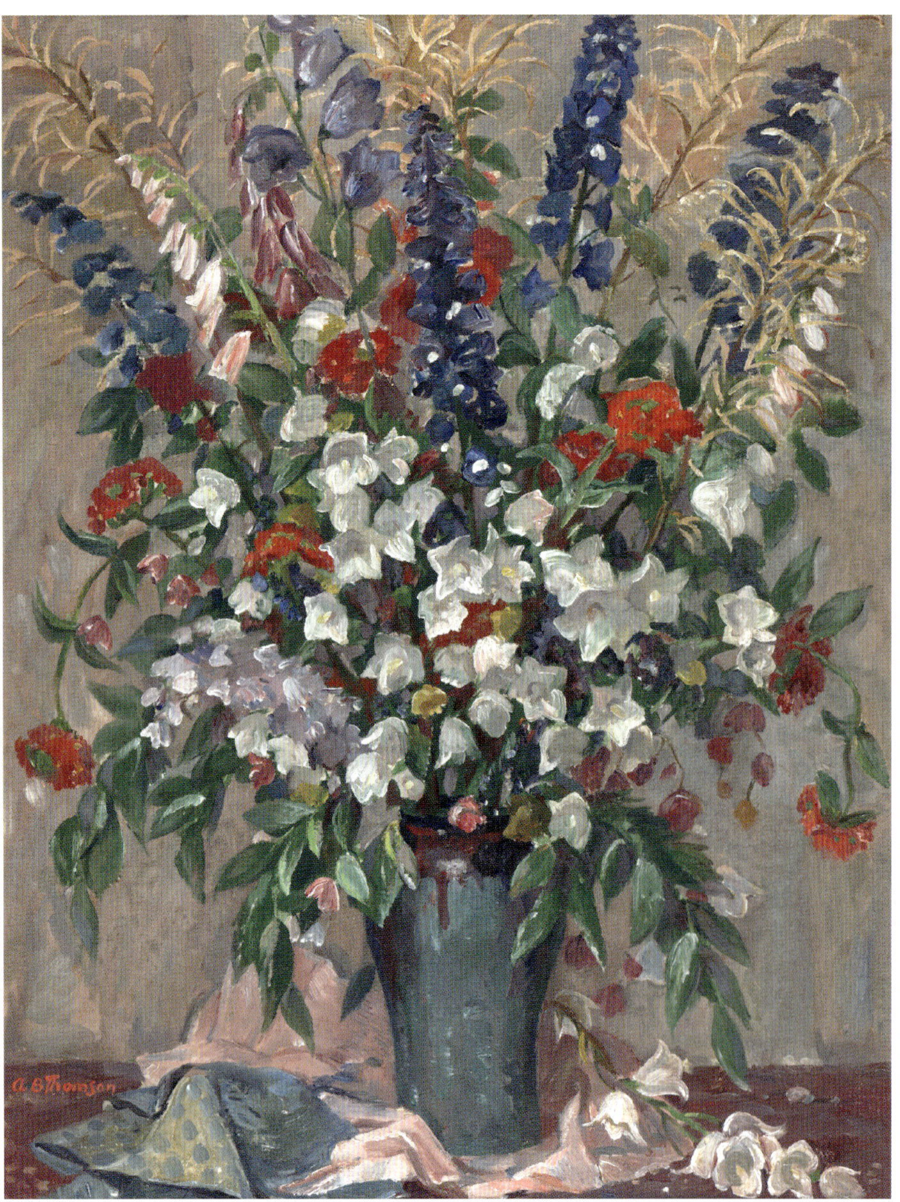

Plate 27

Flowers
Oil on canvas, *c*.1940
92 x 71cm
Private Collection
(Photograph: Antonia Reeve)

From the early 1940s onwards, bouquets of flowers became an increasingly common theme in Thomson's still-life paintings. This example conveys a joyful sense of abundance, with blooms reaching towards the edges of the canvas and cascading onto the drapery below. The turquoise vase was a favourite piece of the artist and his wife; it features in several compositions.

Plate 28

Professor Norman Kemp Smith (1872–1958)
Oil on canvas, 1946
100 x 85cm
The University of Edinburgh
(Photograph: The University of Edinburgh)

Dundee-born philosopher Norman Kemp Smith held the Chair of Logic and Metaphysics at the University of Edinburgh from 1919 until 1945. This formal portrait was one of two that Thomson was commissioned to deliver to mark the professor's retirement. Both versions show Kemp Smith holding a book, with the University crest on the curtain behind him. This is the larger of the pair, which was intended to be displayed on campus.

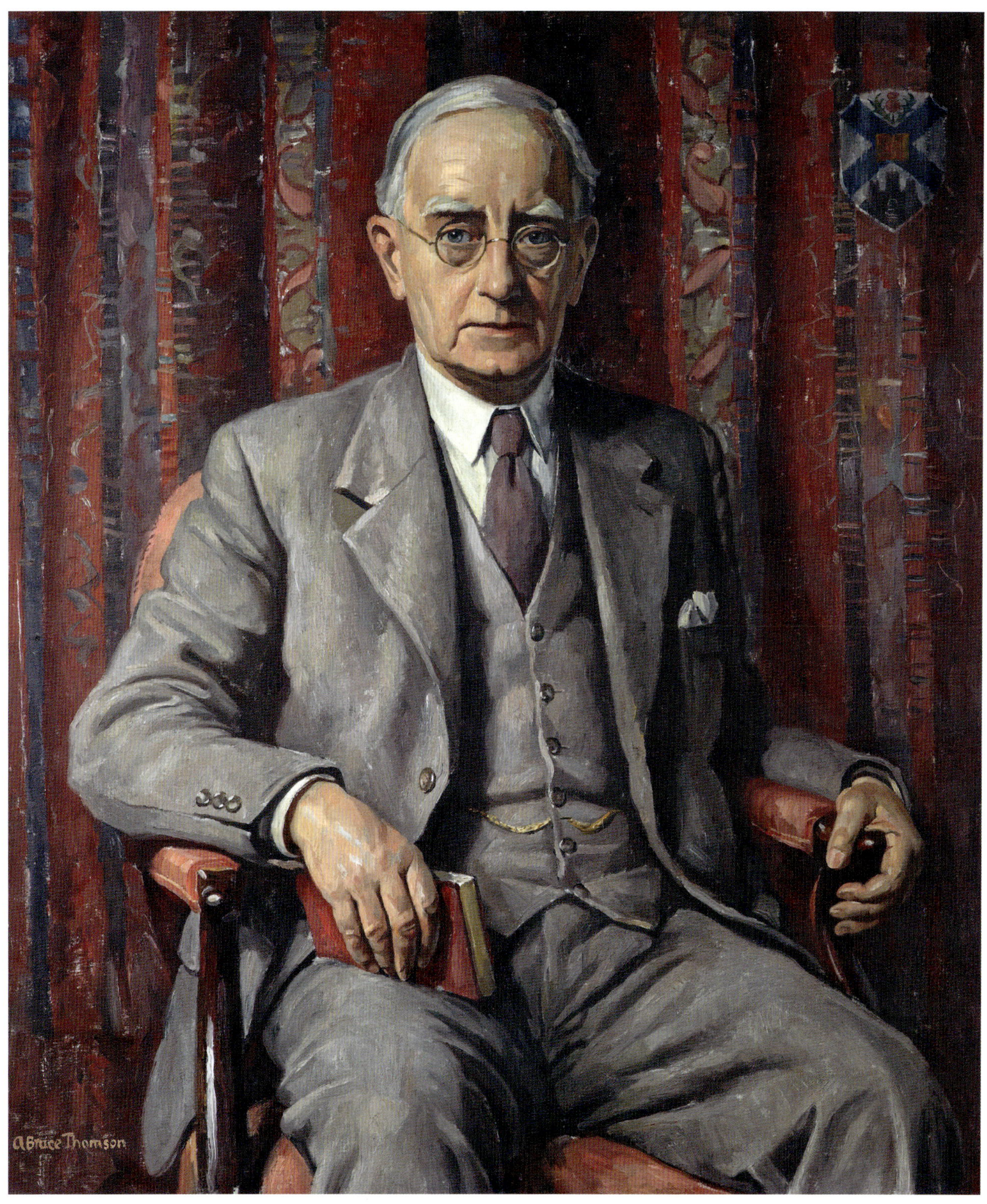

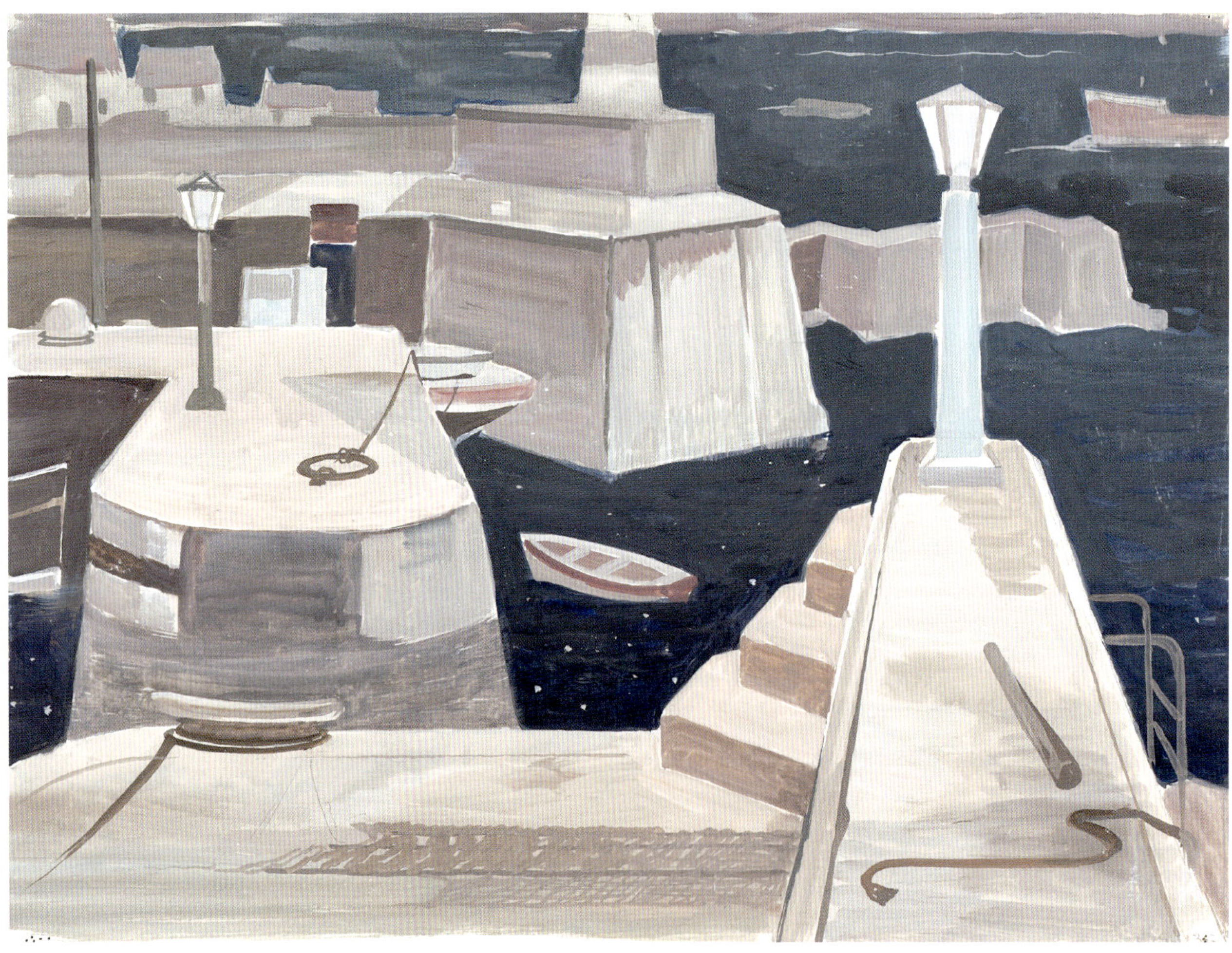

This is a preparatory study for *Harbour, St Abbs*, an oil painting now owned by the National Galleries of Scotland. The east coast fishing communities of Eyemouth and St Abbs held a long-running fascination for Thomson, who enjoyed the challenge of depicting complex harbour scenes. As he remarked to his friend D.M. Sutherland: 'St Abbs harbour at first sight looks that it would be paintable – I daresay it is but it takes some sorting out.'

In the mid-1940s Thomson visited Shieldaig in Wester Ross. The remote village received few tourists at the time and he was charmed by its quiet, picturesque setting.

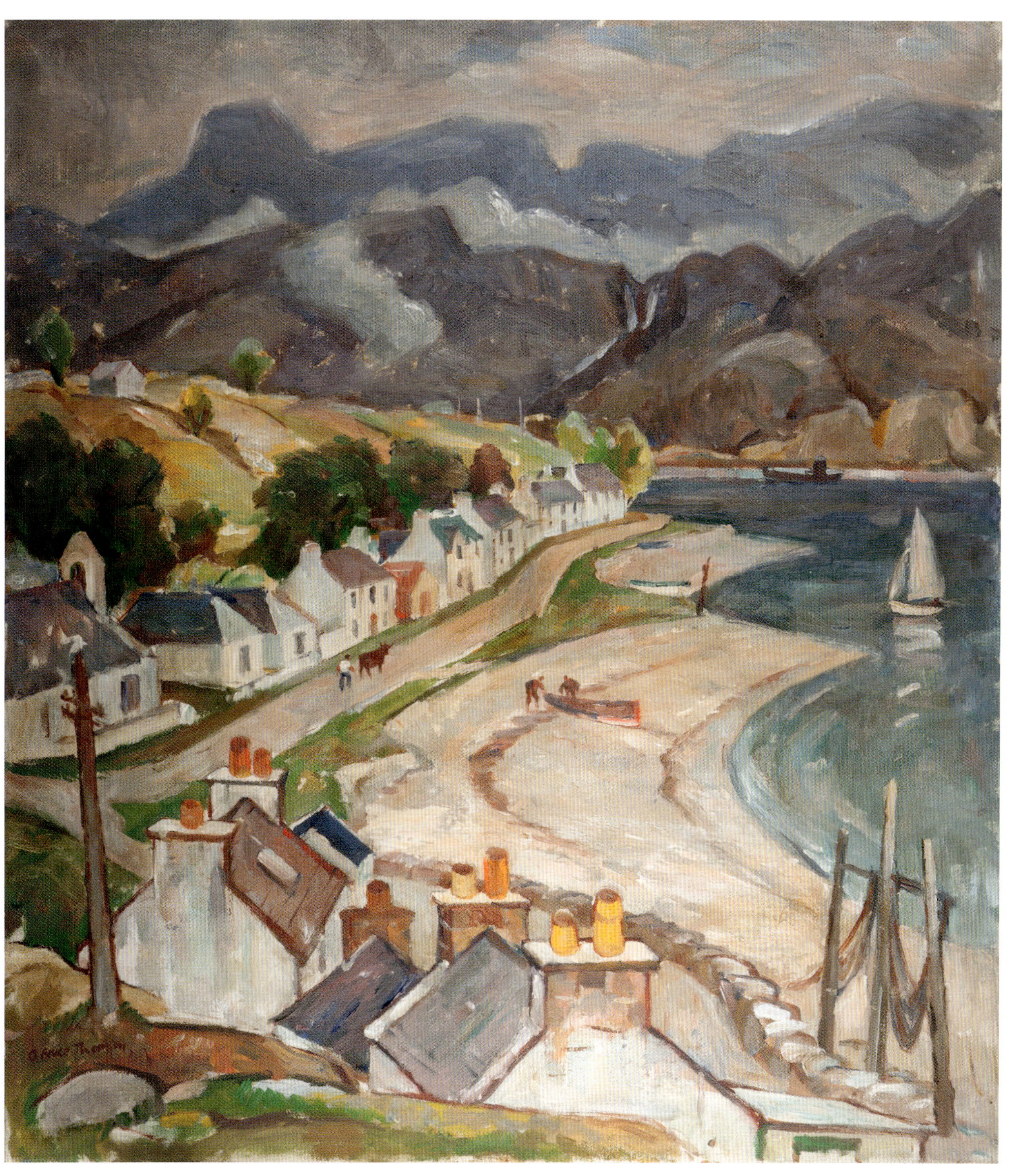

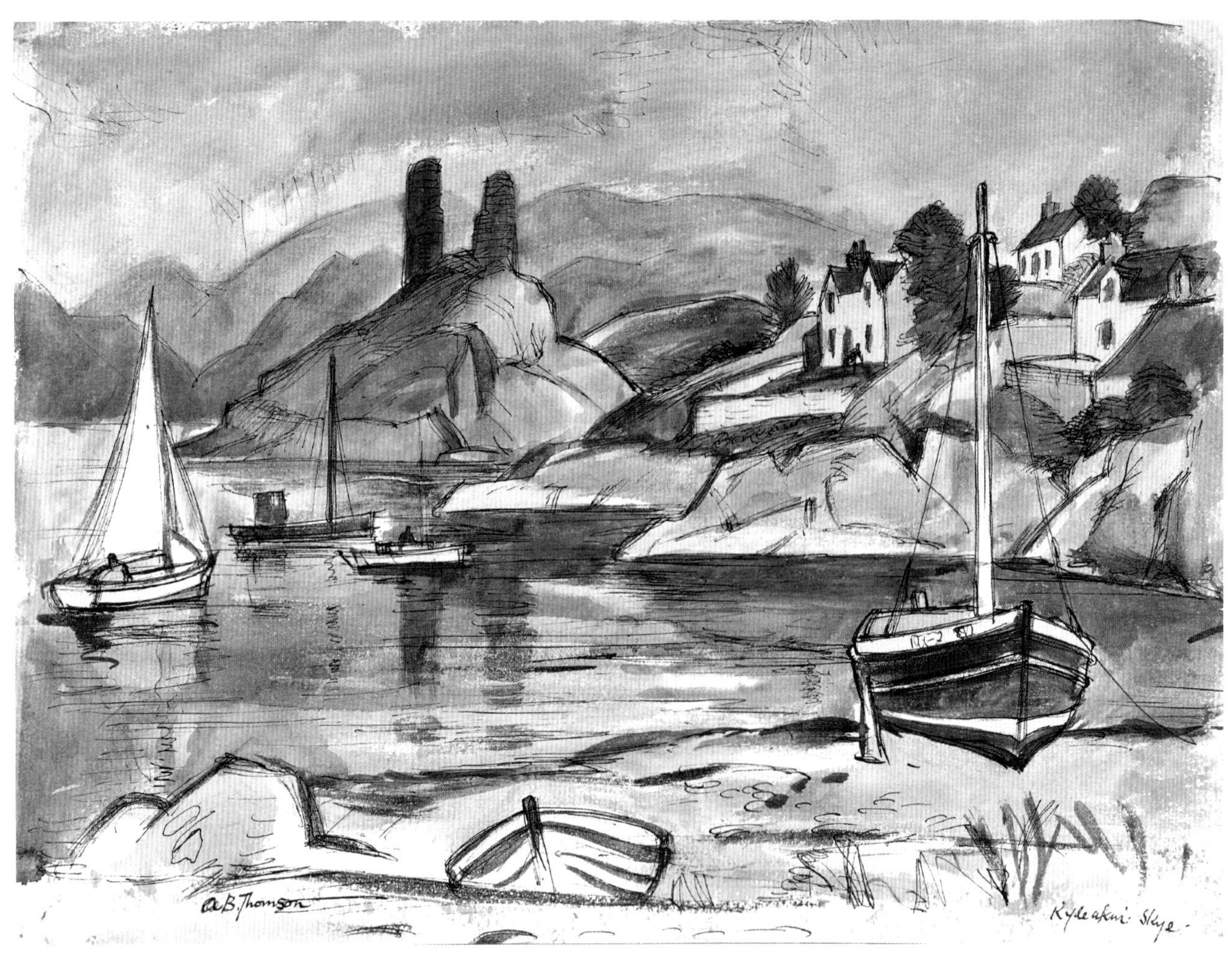

Plate 31

Kyleakin, Skye
Ink and wash on paper, unknown date
28 x 38cm
Private Collection
(Photograph: The Scottish Gallery)

Thomson produced images of the Isle of Skye throughout
his career, using a range of media to achieve different effects.
This monochrome study was executed with ink and wash,
a technique in which water is applied to soften linear forms
and add tone. The contrast between light and dark emphasises
the dramatic atmosphere of Caisteal Maol, the ruined fortress
overlooking the bay.

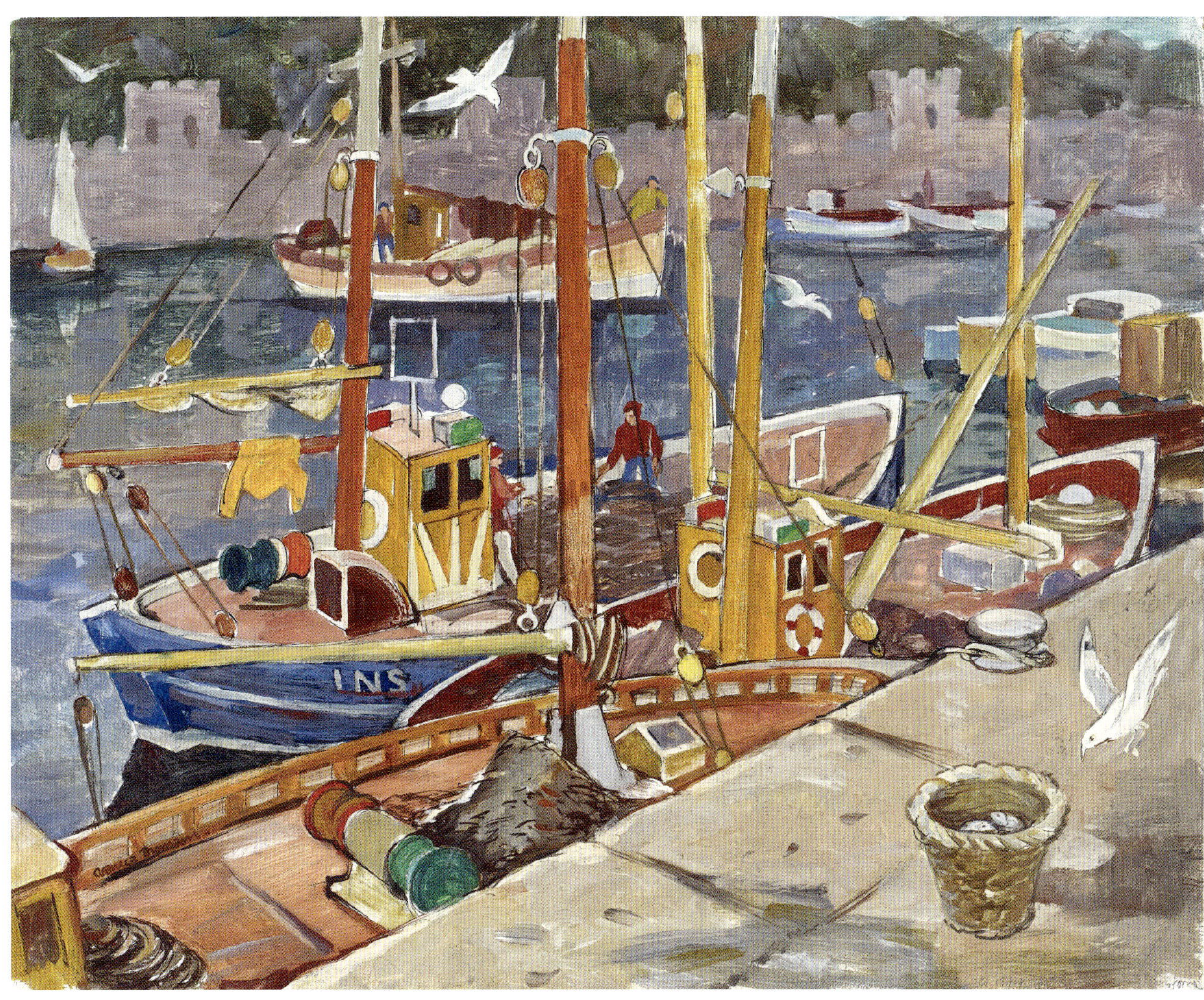

PLATE 32

Stornoway Harbour
Tempera on board, *c.*1954
51 x 63.5cm
Private Collection
(Photograph: The Scottish Gallery)

In this playful scene Thomson recreates the bustling character
of Stornoway harbour in the Outer Hebrides. Fishermen
labour over their nets, while gulls swoop around in search of
unguarded spoils. The artist made several trips to Lewis during
the 1950s.

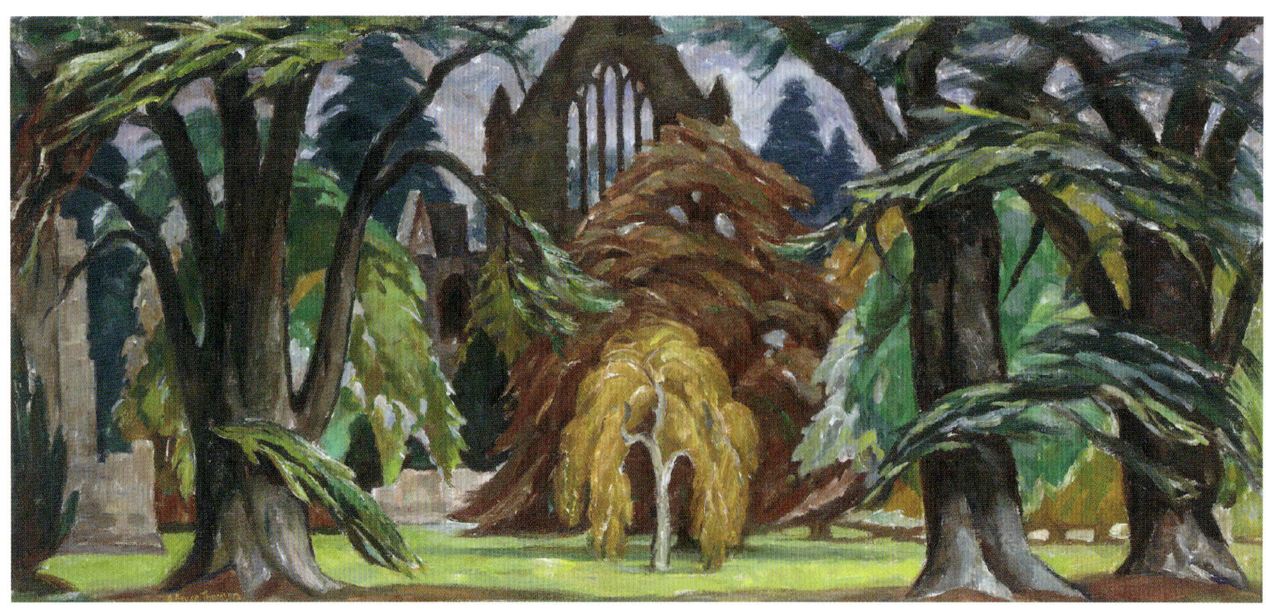

PLATE 33

Park and Ruined Abbey
Oil on canvas, *c.*1961
58.1 x 127cm
Royal Scottish Academy. Diploma Collection Deposit, 1961.
(Photograph: Royal Scottish Academy)

In later life, Thomson regularly painted the abbeys of Melrose,
Dryburgh and Kelso in the Scottish Borders. This view of
Dryburgh Abbey among autumn trees was presented to the
Royal Scottish Academy in the early 1960s as his submission
to the RSA Diploma Collection. With its unusual elongated
format and carefully considered balance of formal elements,
this picture demonstrates Thomson's ongoing interest in
compositional structure.

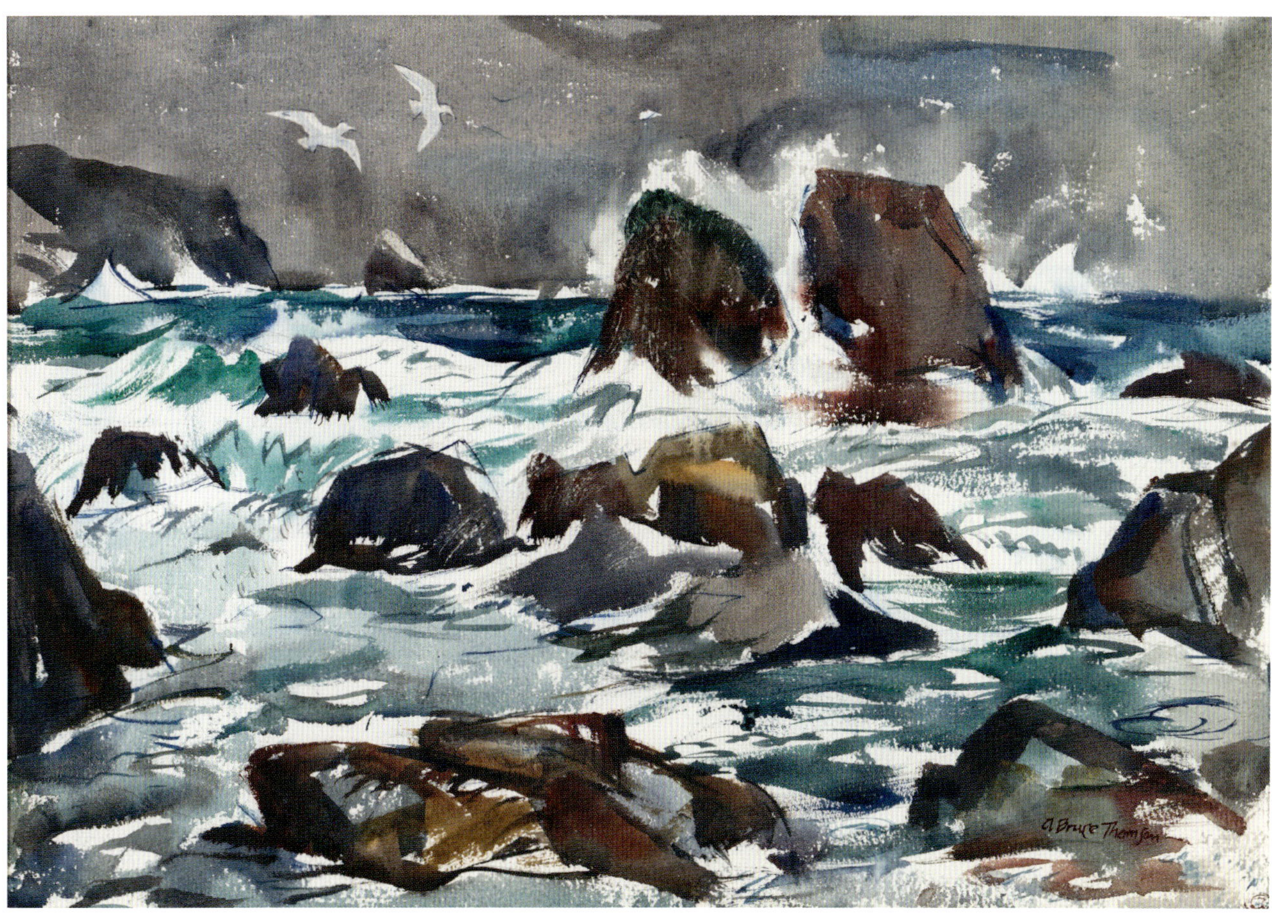

PLATE 34

Stormy Sea
Watercolour on paper, *c*.1963
41.3 x 58.4cm
City Art Centre, City of Edinburgh Museums and Galleries
(Photograph: Antonia Reeve)

Between 1956 and 1963 Thomson served as President of
the Royal Scottish Society of Painters in Watercolour. The
watercolour medium allowed him to work outdoors and create
more instinctively. Here, for example, his depiction of the sea is
loosely handled, with sections of the paper left bare to suggest
the movement of foaming waves. The overall effect is one of
spontaneity and direct experience.

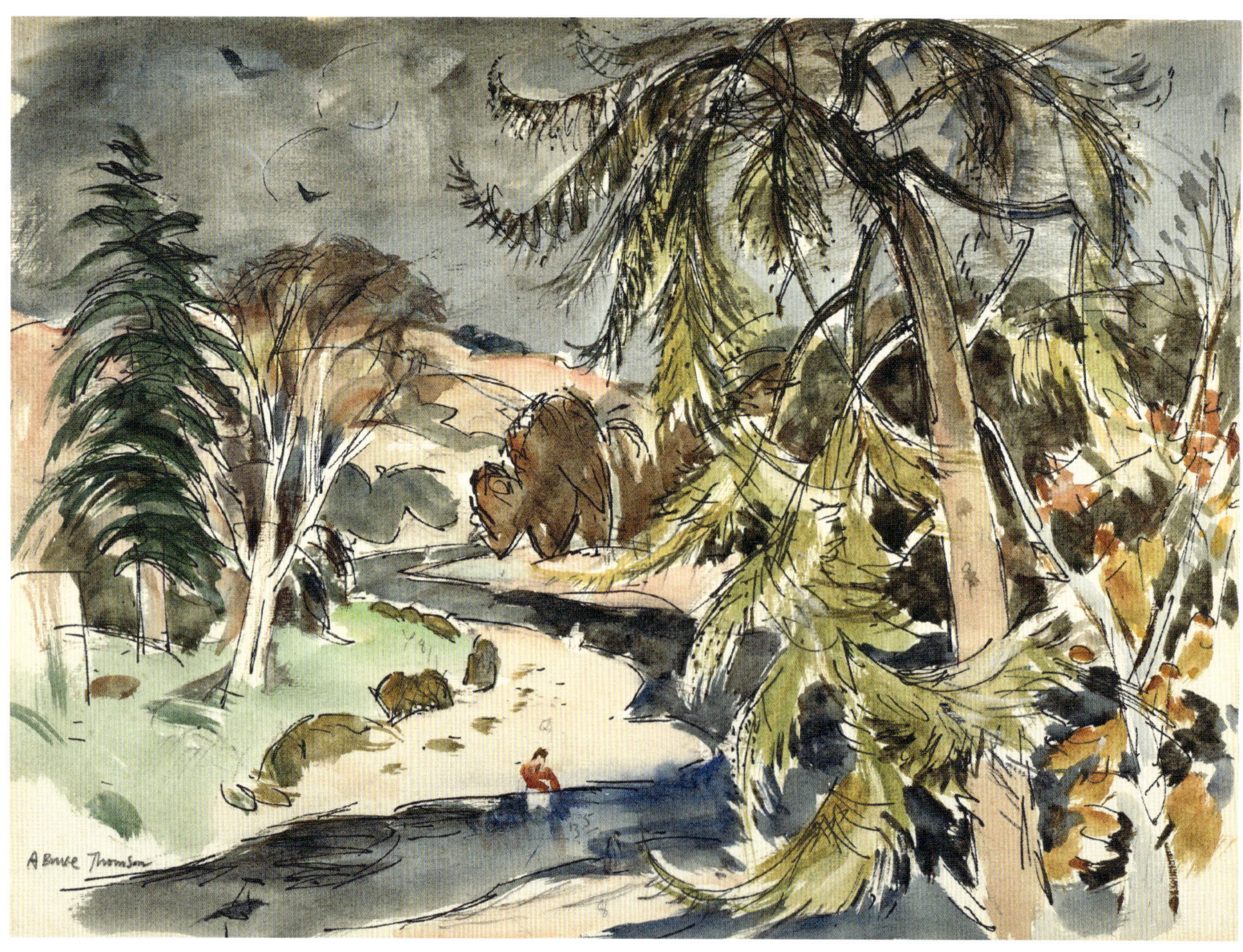

Plate 35

The River Tweed above Melrose
Ink and watercolour on paper, before 1966
32 x 42cm
City Art Centre, City of Edinburgh Museums and Galleries
(Photograph: Antonia Reeve)

Although Thomson lived in the city all his life, he loved walking
and sketching in rural locations. Whenever he spent long
periods in his Edinburgh studio, he found himself 'champing
at the bit' to return to the countryside. This spot on the River
Tweed, near the Lowood estate at Melrose, was somewhere that
inspired him repeatedly.

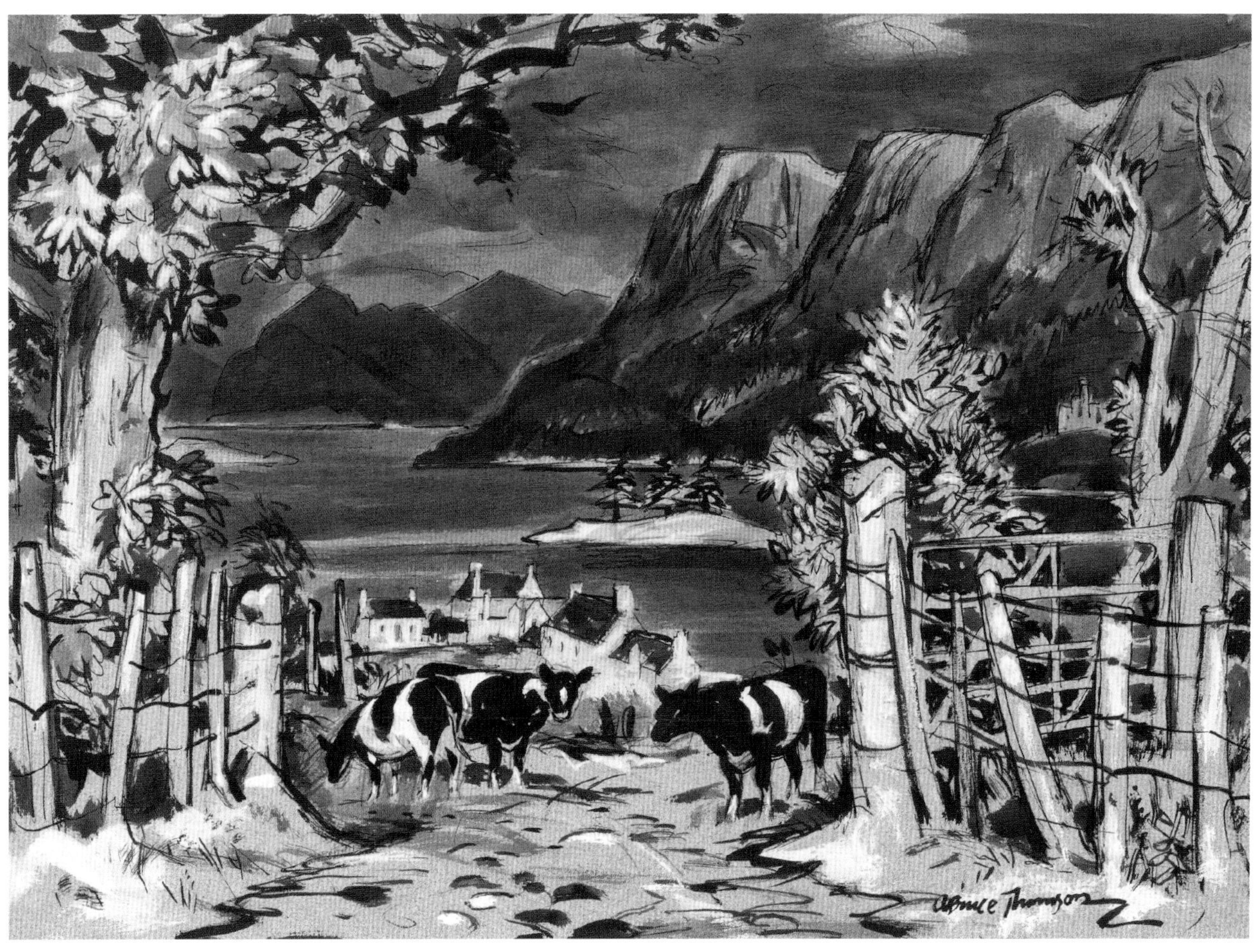

PLATE 36

Loch Carron, Passing Storm
Ink and wash on paper, *c*.1964
33.7 x 45.5cm
Royal Scottish Academy. David Muirhead Memorial Fund
Purchase, 1964.
(Photograph: Royal Scottish Academy)

This ink and wash landscape provides an elevated view of
Plockton in Wester Ross, with the headland of Duncraig
rising steeply in the distance. Thomson painted extensively
in this area in the 1960s, captivated by the setting and its
unpredictable weather.

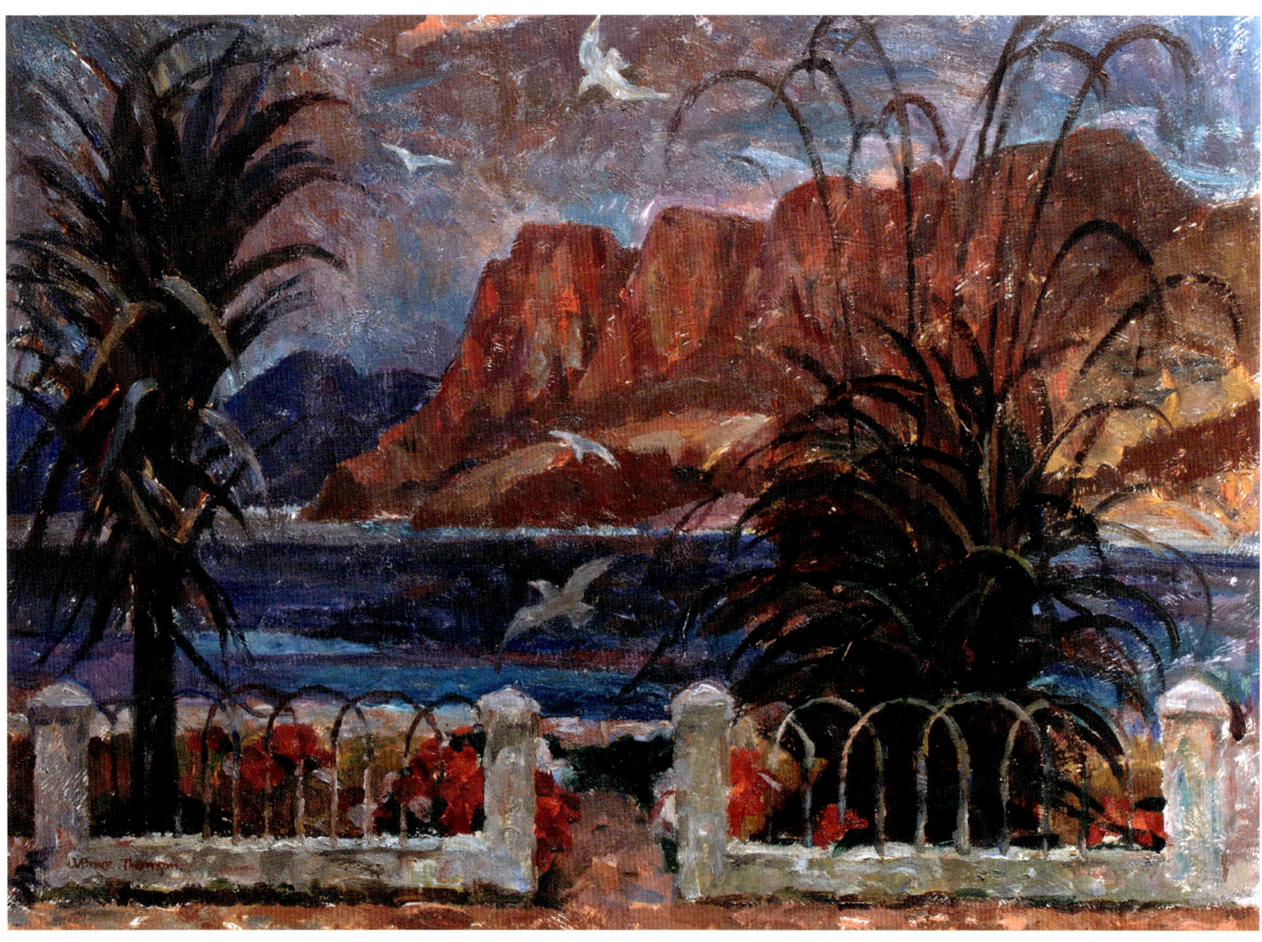

Plate 37

Palm, Pampas Grass and Duncraig
Oil on board, *c.*1967
71.2 x 91.5cm
City Art Centre, City of Edinburgh Museums and Galleries
(Photograph: City Art Centre)

Palm, Pampas Grass and Duncraig is one of Thomson's most celebrated Plockton landscapes.
Having devised a general composition for the painting, he prepared numerous watercolour
sketches in varying colour schemes and levels of detail, before settling on this final version.
In contemporary letters to his friend D.M. Sutherland he alluded to the 'old Plockton magic',
a shorthand for the creative energy they both experienced in this location.

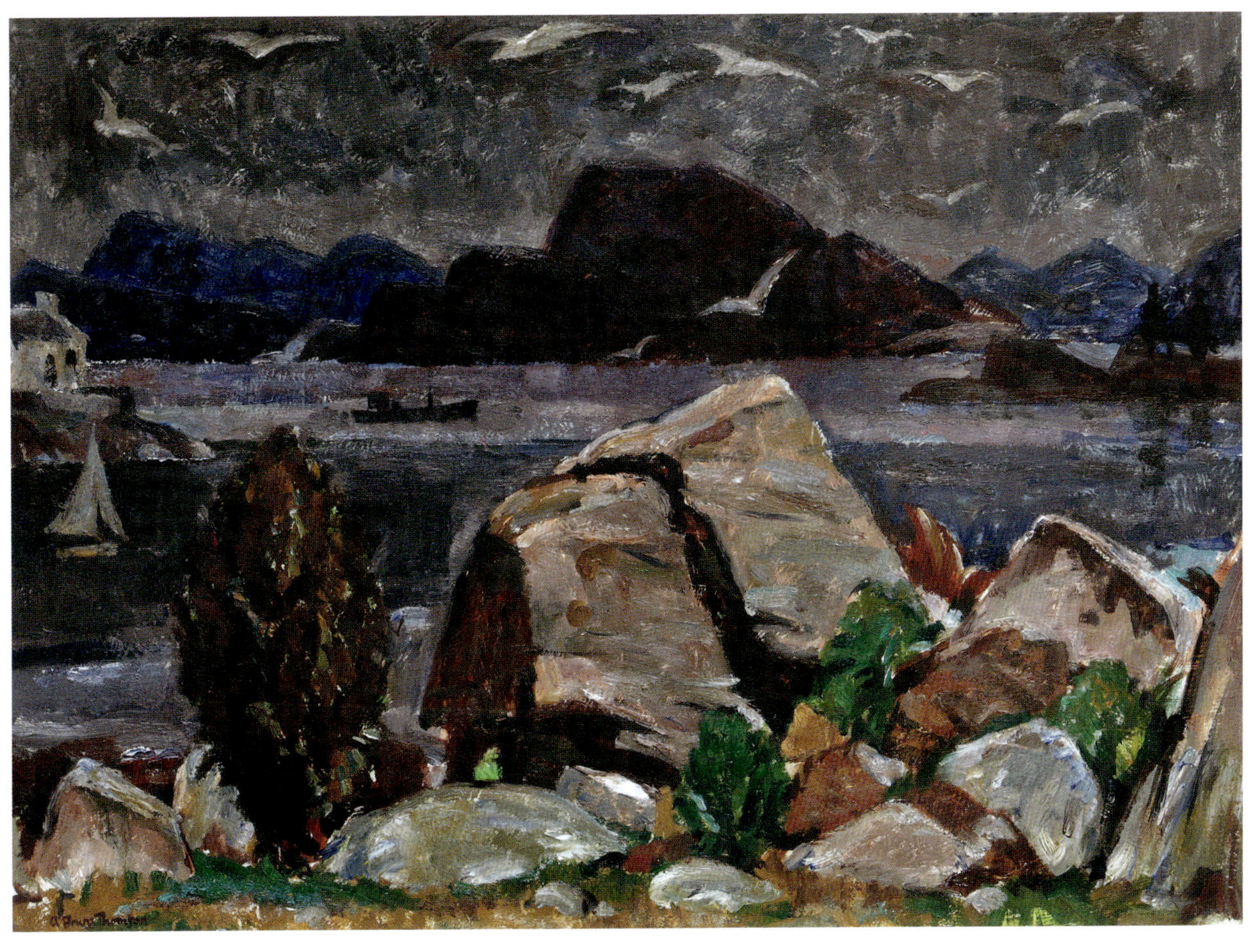

PLATE 38

Loch Carron Shore
Oil on board, *c.*1968
54 × 74.5cm
Royal Scottish Academy. Thomas and Christina Forbes
Hutchison Memorial Fund Purchase, 1968.
(Photograph: Royal Scottish Academy)

Over the course of his career, Thomson showed more than three hundred artworks at the annual exhibitions of the Royal Scottish Academy. This oil painting was displayed there in 1968, when the artist was nearing his mid-eighties.

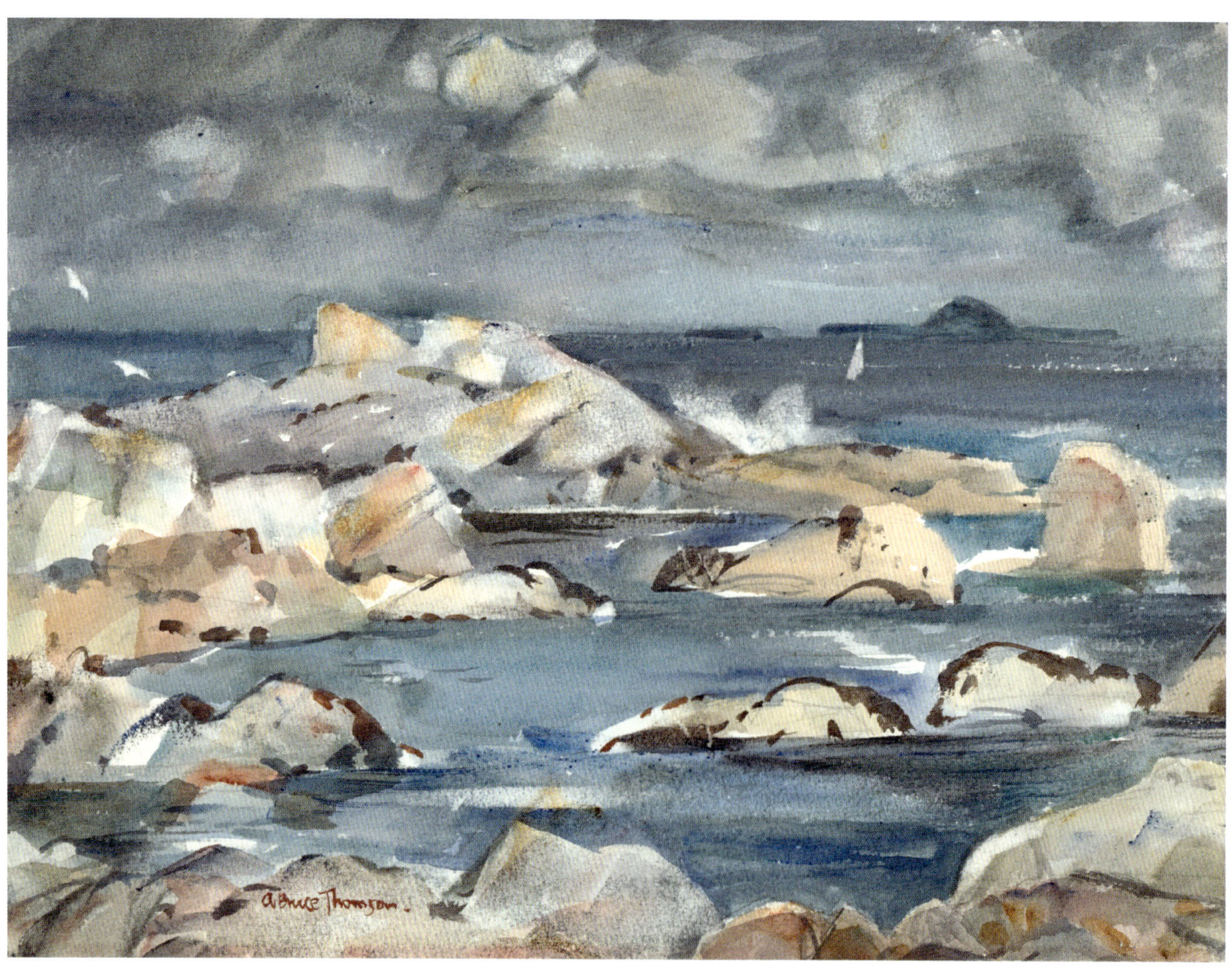

PLATE 39

North End, Iona, in Fitful Sunlight
Watercolour on paper, after 1968
31 x 42cm
City Art Centre, City of Edinburgh Museums and Galleries
(Photograph: Antonia Reeve)

Iona was a popular destination for many Scottish artists in
the mid-twentieth century. Thomson travelled to the island
several times, including a trip in early 1968. On this occasion the
weather was bitterly cold and windy, but he worked prolifically,
completing a series of impressions of the rocky beaches.

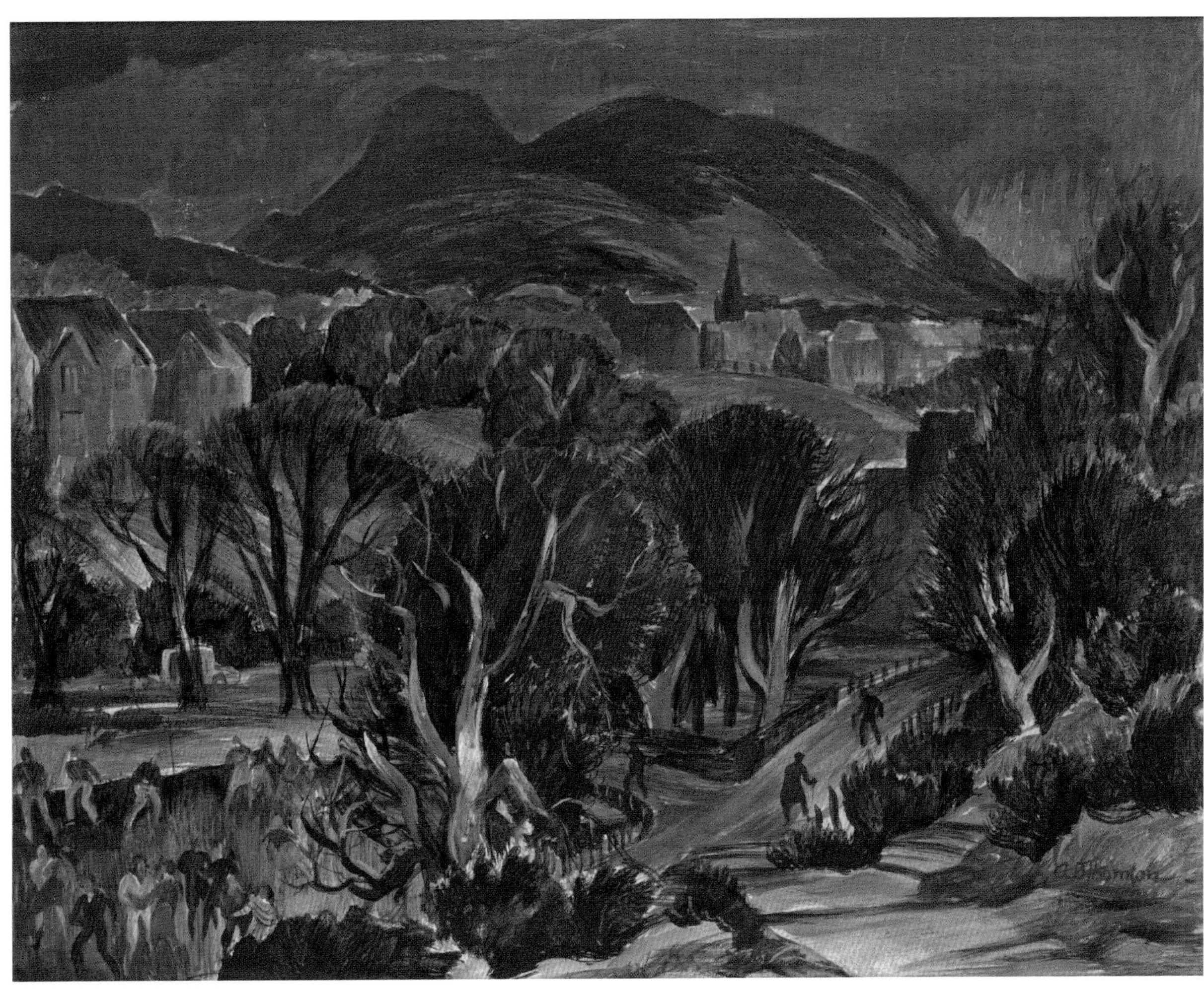

PLATE 40

Edinburgh from Blackford with Skaters on the Pond
Tempera on board, unknown date
49.5 x 61.5cm
Private Collection
(Photograph: Antonia Reeve)

Thomson spent his last decade living in the Blackford area of
Edinburgh. The leafy suburb offered panoramic views towards
Arthur's Seat, a city landmark that became an increasingly
potent motif in his work. He portrayed the hill and its environs
in all seasons and weather conditions, never tiring of the subject.

ADAM BRUCE THOMSON   A TIMELINE

1885	Born in Edinburgh on 22 February
1899–1903	Attends evening classes in Art Department at Heriot-Watt College, Edinburgh
1903–8	Studies at Trustees' School of Art, Edinburgh
1908	Works part-time as temporary Art Master at Royal High School, Edinburgh
1908–9	Studies at Edinburgh College of Art
1909	Receives Architecture Diploma in January
	Exhibits at Royal Scottish Academy (RSA) for the first time
	Awarded Architecture Travelling Scholarship and tours sites in south-east England
	Receives Drawing and Painting Diploma in December
1910	Having been awarded Drawing and Painting Travelling Scholarship, spends time in London, France and Spain
	Appointed to teaching staff at Edinburgh College of Art in October
1911	Visits Orkney and Netherlands
1912–14	Undertakes sketching trips to Dumfries and Galloway area
c.1914	Establishes studio at Synod Hall, Castle Terrace, Edinburgh
1916–18	Serves with Royal Engineers in First World War
1918	Marries Jessie Inglis Hislop on 15 April
1919	Returns to teach at Edinburgh College of Art following war service
	Moves to 149 Warrender Park Road, Edinburgh
	Son Ronald born on 1 November
1921	Daughter Margaret born on 29 April
1924	Daughter Mary born on 6 December
1929	*From My Bedroom Window* purchased for the nation by Scottish Modern Arts Association
1931–3	Spends family holidays with D.M. Sutherland and Dorothy Johnstone in Taynuilt, Argyll
1935	*North Bridge and Salisbury Crags, Edinburgh, from the North West* purchased by Society of Scottish Artists (SSA) and presented to City of Edinburgh
1936–7	Serves as President of SSA
1937	Elected Associate of RSA
1937–8	Spends family holidays on Isle of Lismore, Inner Hebrides
1939–40	Paints 'decorative panel' for Edinburgh Savings Bank
1941	Paints murals for 'The Keel Row' (wartime communal restaurant in Leith)
1945	Commissioned to paint portrait of Professor Norman Kemp Smith
1946	Elected Academician of RSA
	Solo exhibition at Scottish Gallery (Aitken Dott & Son), Edinburgh (21 October–2 November 1946)
1947	Elected Member of Royal Scottish Society of Painters in Watercolour (RSW)
1949–56	Serves as Treasurer of RSA
1950	Retires from teaching at Edinburgh College of Art
c.1950	Visits Tréboul, Brittany
1951–4	Serves on Board of Management for Edinburgh College of Art

1951	Teaches at Stornoway Art Club, Isle of Lewis
1952–5	Serves on Adjudication Committee for Award of Diplomas at Edinburgh College of Art
1956–63	Serves as President of RSW
1960–66	Serves on Adjudication Committee for Award of Diplomas at Edinburgh College of Art
1963	Awarded OBE in New Year Honours List
1965	Moves to 65 Cluny Gardens, Edinburgh
1967	Solo exhibition at Scottish Arts Club, Edinburgh (late January–mid-March 1967) Solo exhibition at Douglas & Foulis Gallery, Edinburgh (20 May–3 June 1967)
1971	Becomes Honorary Retired Member of RSA
1976	*Rising Moon: Arthur's Seat* wins William J. Macaulay Award at RSA Dies in Edinburgh on 4 December

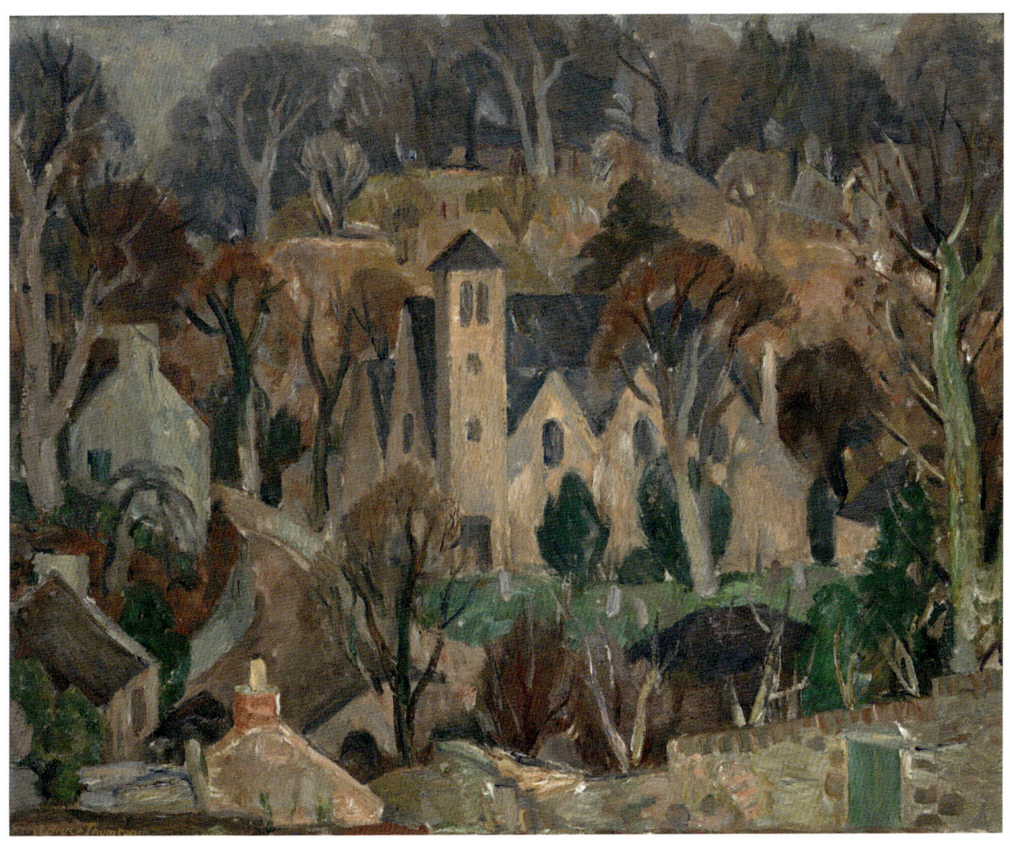

Adam Bruce Thomson, *Church in the Valley*, c.1950. Private Collection. © The artist's estate.
(Photograph: Antonia Reeve)

ACKNOWLEDGEMENTS

Thank you to the following individuals and organisations who have assisted and supported the author throughout the research and writing of this publication: Sir Alexander McCall Smith CBE; Lesley Winton; Joyce Kelly; Antonia and Indigo Reeve; Barry Arnott; Duncan Macmillan; David Patterson and Maeve Toal (City Art Centre, Edinburgh); Tommy Zyw and Sophie Lawson (Scottish Gallery, Edinburgh); Sandy Wood and Robin Rodger (Royal Scottish Academy of Art and Architecture); Patrick Elliott, Kerry Horsburgh and Jacqueline Austin (National Galleries of Scotland); Anna Hawkins, Morven Rodger and the staff at the Centre for Research Collections, University of Edinburgh; Heidi Egginton, Sally Todd and the staff at the National Library of Scotland; Alice Strang and the staff at Lyon & Turnbull; the Estate of D.M. Sutherland and Dorothy Johnstone; Paul Deaton, Clara Hudson, Ann Kay and Melinda Welch (Sansom & Company); Ian Scott, Liz Scott, Rob Scott and David Scott.

Thank you also to those private collectors and individuals who prefer to remain anonymous.

Finally, a great many thanks are due to the family of Adam Bruce Thomson. Their knowledge, enthusiasm, generosity and kind hospitality have been invaluable. Without the family's steadfast support and encouragement over the last few years, this publication could not have been realised.

AUTHOR BIOGRAPHIES

Dr Helen E. Scott is Curator of Fine Art at the City Art Centre in Edinburgh. Since 2013 she has been responsible for developing the City of Edinburgh Council's collection of Scottish art, as well as researching and curating temporary exhibitions. She specialises in Scottish art of the nineteenth and twentieth centuries. Previously, she worked as Collections Manager of the Wilhelmina Barns-Graham Trust. She holds a degree in Art History from the University of St Andrews, and completed her PhD there in 2009. Helen has written for a variety of art historical books and journals, and is author of the monographs *Edwin G. Lucas: An Individual Eye* (2018) and *Mary Cameron: Life in Paint* (2019).

Sir Alexander McCall Smith CBE [Foreword] is a novelist and author of more than one hundred books on a wide variety of subjects. He also writes short stories and libretti for composers. Alexander lives in Edinburgh.

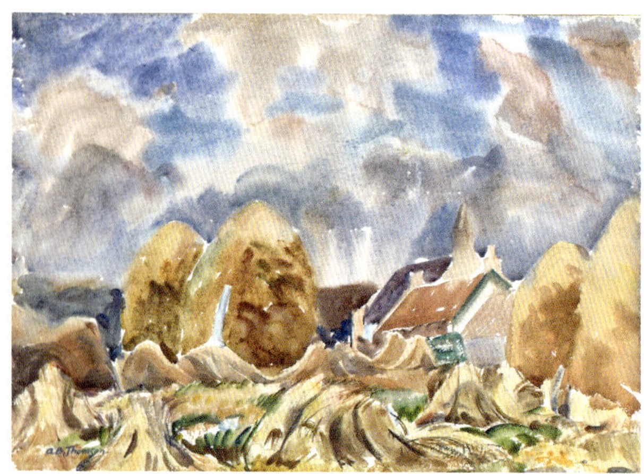

Adam Bruce Thomson, *Stooks, East Lothian*, c.1965.
Private Collection. © The artist's estate.
(Photograph: The Scottish Gallery)